Other Books by Emily Talen

Retrofitting Sprawl: Addressing Seventy Years of Failed Urban Form (Ed.)

The Charter of the New Urbanism, 2nd Edition (Ed.)

Landscape Urbanism and Its Discontents: Dissimulating the Sustainable City (Ed., with Andres Duany)

City Rules: How Regulations Affect Urban Form

Design for Diversity

New Urbanism and American Planning: The Conflict of Cultures

URBAN DESIGN FOR PLANNERS

TOOLS, TECHNIQUES, AND STRATEGIES

EMILY TALEN

PLANETIZEN PRESS

© 2018 by Planetizen, Inc.

Published in the United States by Planetizen Press (www.planetizen.com), an imprint of Planetizen, Inc.

All rights reserved.

No part of this book may be reproduced in any form by any means without permission in writing from the publisher.

Author: Emily Talen
Book design: José Ramirez

ISBN: 9-780990-616245
Library of Congress Control Number: 2018941409

Planetizen is the independent resource for people passionate about urban planning

TO LUC ANSELIN

NOTES ON THE SECOND EDITION

Urban Design for Planners: Tools, Techniques, and Strategies is for anyone who believes that the design of the built environment is central to quality of life in communities of all shapes and sizes, and on every continent.

Structured as a set of ten exercises, the book offers step-by-step instructions on how to observe, analyze, and design functional, civically minded, pedestrian-oriented places. While it is intended for urban planners, architects, landscape architects, geographers, and community activists working in the field, the book could also serve as a text for students in any course that touches on issues of neighborhood, place, and community.

As a companion to the resources offered by *Urban Design for Planners: Tools, Techniques, and Strategies*, Planetizen also offers a series of online videos titled "Urban Design for Planners"(1) on the Planetizen Courses website. Author Emily Talen also instructs all of the courses in the "Urban Design for Planners" series, which was updated with the most recent software applications in 2018.

Packaged together, the book and video series offers the first multimedia urban design curriculum available to the general public.

This book was previously published as *Urban Design Reclaimed: Tools Techniques, and Strategies for Planners* by the American Planning Association's Planners Press in 2009. Planetizen Press has republished the book in its second edition as *Urban Design for Planners: Tools, Techniques, and Strategies*.

(1) The series of online video courses available from Planetizen Courses is available at https://courses.planetizen.com/track/urban-design-planners

CONTENTS

LIST OF FIGURES	X
LIST OF TABLES	XI
ACKNOWLEDGEMENTS	XIII
INTRODUCTION	1
GROUP 1: THE BIGGER PICTURE	13
EXERCISE 1: NEIGHBORHOODS	15
EXERCISE 2: TRANSECTS	25
EXERCISE 3: CONNECTIONS	35
GROUP 2: BASICS	47
EXERCISE 4: CENTERS	49
EXERCISE 5: EDGES	59
EXERCISE 6: MIX	69
EXERCISE 7: PROXIMITY	79
GROUP 3: RECURRENT ISSUES	85
EXERCISE 8: DENSITY	87
EXERCISE 9: PARKING	93
EXERCISE 10: TRAFFIC	101
REFERENCES	108
GLOSSARY	111
DISCUSSION QUESTIONS AND ACTIVITIES	115
INDEX	118

LIST OF FIGURES

I-1.	The Modernist Vision	2
I-2.	List of Symbols Used to Map Design Strategies	7
I-3.	Sketching the Urban Scene	7
I-4.	Sketching the Urban Scene	7
I-5.	Portage Park	11
1-1.	Clarence Perry's Diagram of the "Neighborhood Unit"	16
1-2.	The Livable Neighborhood	16
1-3.	The Transit-Oriented Neighborhood	16
1-4.	Quarter-mile "Pedestrian Sheds"	17
1-5.	A Weakly Defined Intersection	17
1-6.	The Official Neighborhoods of Portage Park	18
1-7.	Census Tracts Used as Proxies for Neighborhoods	18
1-8.	Police Precincts in Portage Park	19
1-9.	Population Density and Commercial Land in Delineating Neighborhoods	19
1-10.	Potential Neighborhood Edges and Existing Commercial Uses	19
1-11.	Traditional Central Places: Parks, Schools, and Major Institutions	19
1-12.	The Hierarchy of Streets in Portage Park	20
1-13.	A Combination of Layers: Centers, Neighborhoods, and Precincts	20
1-14.	Another Combination: Centers, Neighborhoods, and Density	20
1-15.	Another Combination: Centers, Commercial Areas, and Edges	20
1-16.	One Possible Set of Neighborhoods	21
1-17.	Another Possible Set of Neighborhoods	21
2-1.	Transect Zones: from Rural to Urban	26
2-2.	Transect Zone Specifications Regarding Form and Use	26
2-3.	Dissect Analysis	27
2-4.	Twenty-eight Zoning Categories in Portage Park	29
2-5.	Blocks near Major Thoroughfares	30
2-6.	Population Density by Block	30
2-7.	Existing Land-Use Intensity	31
2-8.	Proposed Transect Zones for Portage Park	31
2-9.	Public Versus Private Frontage	32
2-10.	Transect Zones and Building Form	32
3-1.	Block Types: Square, Elongated, Irregular	35
3-2.	Clusters of Regional Facilities and Routes	36
3-3.	"Hotspots" of Connectivity Problems	36
3-4.	Poor Connectivity to Neighborhood Centers	37
3-5.	Clusters of Activity Spaces	37
3-6.	Improved Regional Connectivity: Area 1	38
3-7.	Gateway to Portage Park	38
3-8.	Improved Regional Connectivity: Area 2	38
3-9.	Improved Regional Connectivity: Area 3	39
3-10.	Improved Connectivity: The Cul-de-sac.	40
3-11.	Improved Connectivity: A Multigenerational Park Connecting Diverse Housing Areas	40
3-12.	Improved Connectivity: A Square Enlivens Small Retail	40
3-13.	Improved Connectivity: Breaking Through a "Clogged Artery"	41
3-14.	Improved Connections to the Center	42
3-15.	Alleys as Pleasant Pedestrian Pathways	42
3-16.	Activity Clusters: Strip Mall Activation	43
3-17.	Activity Clusters: Improving the Corridor with Active Uses	43
3-18.	Activity Clusters: A Pivotal Point Between Two Public Realms	44
3-19.	Activity Clusters: Street Upgrades Around a Church Complex	44
4-1.	Types of Civic Spaces	49
4-2.	Different Types of Neighborhood Centers in Portage Park	50
4-3.	Neighborhood Center in Portage Park	50
4-4.	Neighborhood Center in Portage Park	50
4-5.	Schools as Centers	52
4-6.	Parks as Centers	52
4-7.	Commercial Areas as Centers	52
4-8.	Publicly Owned Land Where New Centers Could Be Created	52
4-9.	School Site as a Neighborhood Center	54
4-10.	European Parking Areas That Also Serve Civic Functions	54
4-11.	School Site as a Neighborhood Center	54
4-12.	Parks as Centers: The Entrance	54
4-13.	Parks as Centers: Connections and Focal Points	55
4-14.	Commercial Areas as Centers	56
4-15.	A Statue in the Center of an Intersection	56
4-16.	New Centers: Capitalize on a Cluster of Publicly Owned Buildings	56
5-1.	An Artfully Designed Cloverleaf Intersection	59
5-2.	Transportation Corridors and Industrial Sites	60
5-3.	Large Vacant Parcels and Large Parks	60
5-4.	Main Edges in Portage Park	60
5-5.	Internal Edges with Connectivity Problems	60
5-6.	Edges and Neighborhood Boundaries	61
5-7.	A Strong Edge Adjacent to Incompatible Uses	61
5-8.	Two Types of Edges: Filters and Seams	62
5-9.	An Edge Area in Portage Park	62
5-10.	Three Types of Filters and Three Types of Seams	62
5-11.	Binding Two Sides of a Strong Edge	63
5-12.	Integrating an Industrial Corridor	63
5-13.	Integrating a "Trapped" Residential Area	64

5-14.	Inserting a Greenway and Connecting Two Small Parks	64
5-15.	Adding Resilient Uses	64
5-16.	Bike Path Embracing the Edge	66
6-1.	Land-Use Mix by Parcel	70
6-2.	Housing-Type Mix by Census Block Group	70
6-3.	Housing-Type Mix by Parcel	70
6-4.	Housing-Type Mix by Parcel and Census	70
6-5a-c.	Modest Interventions to Sustain and Bind the Mix	72
6-6.	Upgrading Parking Lots Attached to Nonresidential Buildings	73
6-7.	Strategies to Support High Housing-Type Mix	73
6-8.	Neighborhood Pocket Park System	73
6-9.	Anchoring a Key Intersection in a High-Mix Area	74
6-10.	Underlying Diversity: Building Age	74
6-11.	Underlying Diversity: Number of Stories	76
6-12.	Infill Strategies	76
6-13.	Bungalow Court	76
7-1.	Areas with Good Access to Parks, Schools, and Libraries	79
7-2.	Spatial Patterns of Sociodemographic Variables in Portage Park	80
7-3.	Areas with High Need and Low Proximity	80
7-4.	Vacant Lots in the Commercial Area	80
7-5.	Commercial Infill	81
7-6.	Strategically Placed Public Amenities	82
8-1.	Housing Infill Strategies, Early 20th Century	87
8-2.	Parcels Close to Civic Spaces	88
8-3.	Parcels Close to Transit and Commercial Uses	88
8-4.	Available Space: Open Land Near Civic, Transit, and Commercial Uses	88
8-5.	Available Space by Transect Zone	88
8-6.	Portage Park: Available Space by Transect Zone	89
8-7.	Housing Infill Strategies and Corresponding Transect Zones	91
8-8.	Increasing Density Based on Transect Intensity Levels	91
9-1.	Creative Car Storage	93
9-2.	Humanizing a Parking Lot	94
9-3.	Parking Buffered By Planting	94
9-4.	Parking Above and Retail Below	94
9-5.	Land Given Over to the Storage of Cars	94
9-6.	Four Options For Solving the Parking Lot Problem	96
9-7.	High-Usage Lot with Public Space Nearby	96
9-8.	Eliminate the Lot	97
9-9.	Reconfigure the Street	98
9-10.	Convert the Lot Using Small Retail	98
9-11.	Convert a Cluster of Lots Using Small Retail	98
9-12.	Buffer the Lot	98
10-1.	Streets That Carry Local and Through Traffic	102
10-2.	Wide Streets with Insufficient Pedestrian Realms	102
10-3.	Streets Carrying Local and Through Traffic	104
10-4.	Three Traffic Issues	104
10-5.	Traffic Calming in Area 1	104
10-6.	Thoroughfare Redesign: A Boulevard Street	104
10-7.	Axonometric View of the Boulevard Street	105

LIST OF TABLES

Table I-1. Design Elements	1
Table I-2. Selected Census 2000 Statistics for the Portage Park Community Area	10
Table 2-1. Transect Zone Descriptions for Portage Park	29
Table 2-2. Rules for Transect Zone Assignment	31
Table 2-3. The Synoptic Survey	33

Toronto, Canadaz
Credit: Leaside Bridge

ACKNOWLEDGMENTS

This book is the result of many years' worth of thinking about the role of urban planners in urban design. It started when I was in graduate school in the city planning program at Ohio State University, where, in the 1980s, planning students were taught to design new towns using colored markers. Looking back, it was not a bad approach, and Professor Larry Gerckens made it all seem real by connecting our efforts to those of an earlier generation of planners. It is no coincidence that Gerckens taught both new town design and city planning history.

From there, I worked in the "advanced planning" section of the City of Santa Barbara for about six years. There my boss was Dave Davis, whom I thank for the many lessons I learned from him about the importance of design, place, and politics. My first project was an analysis of what the appropriate parking requirements for a bed and breakfast inn should be in an "R-O" zone. Santa Barbara is the kind of place that obsesses about such things, but you have to admit the town is worth it.

A special thanks to Konrad Perlman for helping out initially and getting the ideas for this book flowing. I started writing this book while I was at the University of Illinois, and there I thank especially Varkki George Pallathucheril, Samantha Singer, Jason Brody, Chris Silver, and Lew Hopkins for their support over the years with urban design matters. In Arizona, I thank Elif Tural for her help with some of the graphics. Thanks to Dan and Karen Parolek for sharing some of their SketchUp models. The staff at APA and Planners Press, especially Sylvia Lewis, Timothy Mennel, Joanne Shwed, and Michael Sonnenfeld have been very supportive (and patient) throughout the production process.

But most of all, I once again thank my friends in the new urbanist community, from whom I have learned a great deal about the importance of design. New urbanism and new urbanists continue to be misunderstood, especially in the academic circles in which I operate. People outside of the discussion do not seem to recognize the depth of the internal debate that revolves around the issues of place, design, sustainability, the human spirit, and social justice. No other group is so impassioned about these connections.

I want to thank especially Sandy Sorlien, Laura Hall, Ann Daigle, Andres Duany, David Brain, Michael Mehaffy, Steve Mouzon, Ellen Dunham-Jones, Bruce Donnelly, John Anderson, Jennifer Hurley, Bill Spikowski, John Norquist, Payton Chung, Patrick Pinnell, Peter Swift, Ray Gindroz, Laurie Volk, Philip Bess, Sara Hines, Shelley Poticha, Tom Low, Laurence Aurbach, Lizz Plater-Zyberk, Rick Bernhardt, Chuck Bohl, Stefanos Polyzoides, John Massengale, Rob Steuteville, Doug Farr, and Phil Langdon. All of them, and others I've undoubtedly (and unintentionally) missed, have helped me over the years find answers to the design problems explored in the exercises included in this book. I have always been able to rely on the good folks on the pop-u-list, new-urb, pro-urb, and urbanists listservs for help finding an answer, and I thank them for their sustained commitment to urbanism and urban design. They will not all agree with the approach I have taken in this book, and some will find things to quarrel over, but it is comforting to know that there are people out there who bother to care about such things.

And of course, many thanks to my family—the extended Talen clan, the Anselins in Belgium, and especially those who put up with me on a daily basis: Luc, Emma, Lucie, and Thomas Anselin.

Perdana Botanical Gardens, Kuala Lumpur, Malaysia
Credit: Izuddin Helmi Adnan

INTRODUCTION

"Human settlements are structured into private and public realms, whatever their purpose, size or location. Yet, neither public nor private enterprise generate a robust and elegant public realm as a mere by-product of their activities. Its beauty, its socializing power are the fruit of conscious intent, of civilizing vision."

Leon Krier, The Architectural Tuning of Settlements, 2008

THERE ARE TWO KINDS OF URBAN DESIGN

The first kind is done by architects. It treats urban design like a big architectural project—a simultaneously designed group of buildings and public spaces. The approach is mostly concerned with the arrangement of three-dimensional objects in space: massing, texture, materials, and the unique designs of individual buildings and spaces. It is generally all of one conception and driven by a monied client like a private developer or a municipal government. It is the kind of large-scale urban design going on in places such as Beijing and Dubai by big-name architects working for big-time developers. It is corporate, consumer-driven, often glamorous, and resource-intensive.

The other kind of urban design is community-based. It is rooted in the urban planning profession rather than architecture, and has a much more distinctly social purpose in mind. It is focused on the health of neighborhoods as social units rather than the aesthetic qualities of streetscapes and retail spaces as revenue-generators. It is not developer-driven. It is instead the result of people who care about place coming together and formulating a physical plan for neighborhood improvement. It is about procuring the best and most aesthetically pleasing places for all kinds of people, weaving together the varied services, functions, economic activities, and environmental protection they require.

There is a time and place for each of these urban design approaches. This book is motivated by the second approach—the one more akin to urban planning than architecture.

RECLAIMING URBAN DESIGN

This book is aimed at broadening urban design to reach beyond the domain of architects. If planners are to help develop communities that function well, accommodate different types of people, promote a sense of caring about place, and ultimately provide a more supportive and inspiring public realm, they need to be actively engaged in the urban design process, assisting communities in their efforts to find a collective, "civilizing vision," to use Leon Krier's phrase.

While most architects would agree that urban design is more than the design of groups of buildings or sections of streets, there is a fundamental truth about urban design that sometimes gets swept under the designer's rug. Neighborhood design must simultaneously support social, environmental, and economic purposes before it serves artistic inspiration. Design that is poignant or idiosyncratic often makes for great architecture, but, in the realm of design for neighborhoods and communities, design serves a different purpose. This creates a dilemma for architects who have been taught to seek out exceptions to the rule as sources for inspiration. Urban design that focuses on helping neighborhoods become better places to live may be much more about instilling time-honored regularities than searching for ways to employ novelty.

The design interventions proposed in this book are first and foremost motivated by civic concern—design that supports diverse, sustainable, vibrant, and equitable communities. Proposals to connect two spaces, insert a public park, route a path in a certain direction, focus attention on a particular intersection—all of these are supported by an underlying social logic focused on creating healthy neighborhoods and communities. It is the kind of design that values the common good and the public realm ahead of the bottom line.

Related to this, the book is intended to help urban planning regain confidence in the realm of urban design. Somewhere around the mid-20th century, planning as a profession lost its focus on the importance of a "civilizing vision." Some blame the experience of urban renewal, which had the effect of recasting the fields of both architecture and planning away from a design-based concern for civic health. Witold Rybczynski has argued that, after the 1960s, architecture stopped talking about social goals and returned to its function as the avant garde, "exchanging the role of environmental designer for that of fashion maven," while planning recast itself as a profession of negotiators and land-use regulators (Rybczynski, 1999). Unlike architecture, planning did not have building design on which to fall back. Eventually, a "planner" came to be described as "just another person sitting at the table" (Krieger, 1999).

Yet, in the last few years, motivated by antisprawl activism, there has been growing recognition that the loss of connection between planning and design has had dire consequences for the American built landscape. While the design-planning nexus is still masked by zoning regulation, socioeconomic analysis, and the rules of bureaucracies, planners seem more aware now than ever that many of the things they control have profound design consequences. There is realization that something as mundane as a zoning code or the regulation of a parking lot can have lasting effects on place quality.

With this recognition, planners are poised to take the lead on relating matters of design to critical social objectives. Freed from the burden of artistic novelty, they can be the ones adept at using design for civic purposes and social requirements. They can be the ones ensuring that, in the design of human settlements, fundamentals do not get lost in the translation—things like how to make a neighborhood function well, how to support social diversity through design, and how to make a place more civic-minded. They can be the ones ensuring that the creative process of urban design does not obfuscate fundamental needs like sidewalks, aligned frontages, and calmer streets. They can also focus on articulating the rationale behind urban design proposals, rather than trying to argue in favor of one architectural fashion over another. Without having to talk about style, qualities like human scale and equity do not have to appear nostalgic or sentimental.

Architects sometimes have a hard time connecting urban design to social objectives. In many architecture schools, canons, principles, or anything attached to an overt social agenda is viewed suspiciously. The reason is not hard to pinpoint. The application of urban design to social goals like equity has had a rocky translation in the past. The failure of modernist urbanism, with its literal articulation of equality in built form, is now painfully obvious (see **Figure I-1**). Planners themselves did terrible things in the name of social equality, tearing down "blighted" neighborhoods and replacing them with uniform, sterile housing complexes. Add to this the constant emphasis on the zeitgeist of the moment and being "of our time"—which, for "our time," means that truth is relative—and you have little support for the notion that known truths about social needs can inform urban design.

Yet, there are many examples of how the design of the built environment directly affects social objectives. One example is the goal of accommodating multiple types of housing in one neighborhood. Urban design can help make this diversity viable:

- By showing how multifamily units can be accommodated in single-family blocks;
- By designing links between diverse land uses and housing types;
- By creating paths through edges that disrupt connectivity;
- By increasing density near public transit;
- By demonstrating the value of nonstandard unit types like courtyard housing, closes, and residential mews;
- By fitting in small businesses and live/work units in residential neighborhoods;
- By developing codes that successfully accommodate land-use mix;
- By softening the impact of big box development in underinvested commercial strips;
- By designing streets that function as collective spaces; and
- By connecting institutions to their surrounding residential fabric.

In these ways, urban design addresses the basic requirements of human integration, including the fears that arise from uncomfortable proximities, and the often contentious fitting together of wide-ranging uses. Design is needed not to smooth out every potential conflict, but to help make diversity livable, even preferable.

To be able to apply urban design to these kinds of social goals, planners need to reaffirm the importance of urban design and its legitimate place in the urban planning profession. They need to elevate the role of the physical design of place, including not only the three-dimensional qualities of two-dimensional plans but also the way in which design plays a central role in fostering stable, well-functioning, open, and lasting communities. They need to have a fundamental understanding of the principles of good urban design as they relate to neighborhoods and communities. Planners need to emerge out of their focus on the "land-use plan," and instill urban design concepts that have something to say about what places could be like.

This does not mean that they need to become architects. They can cultivate their own sense of urban design, relishing the fact that their profession motivates them to link social, economic, environmental, and aesthetic ideals. It is my hope that this book will help in that effort, putting the design side of planning in a stronger position.

FIGURE I-1

The modernist vision: A literal interpretation of equality in built form. Source: Sert (1944).

APPROACH

While the importance of urban design in planning has been reaffirmed in the past decade, urban planners are lagging behind in their development of the skills necessary to address the basic design needs of a community. This book provides some of the tools planners need to get back in the game. Through a set of 10 exercises, it offers something missing from the urban design literature—a "how-to" book for planners, citizen planners, and anyone with a love for the physical qualities of neighborhoods. It provides an urban design vocabulary and corresponding set of applications that are specifically targeted to nonarchitects. While the focus is on equipping planners with the tools they need to facilitate a community-based approach to urban design, the title of "urban designer" should not be seen in specialist terms. Anyone with time and interest can learn the steps and apply the tools.

The approach is process-oriented, community-based, and proactive. "Process-oriented" means that there are feedback loops and trials and errors, with an emphasis on generating alternatives. It means that it is necessary to thoroughly understand the complexity of an issue before proposing design solutions—especially the social context of a place. Being process-oriented means that there is more than one way of looking at a problem, with more than one solution. It does not mean, however, that outcomes are always unknowable, or that one must steer clear of design interventions that are commonplace, goal-driven, or popular. It only means that there is a certain fluidity to the steps involved in defining a problem and arriving at a solution.

Being "community-based" means that the exercises are intended to give anyone with an interest in the built environment the tools they need to suggest changes and play an active role in its design. Urban design requires a certain level of know-how, but, using the exercises here, anyone can acquire it. Planners and citizen planners (people not necessarily employed as planners but who are active in and have a genuine interest in planning issues) can do all of these exercises.

This book omits the design of specific sites and buildings. There are no tools for landscape plans or building designs. Issues like balance, texture, and composition—so important in the design of a building or specific site—will only occasionally come into play. This should not be considered a limitation. In fact, stopping short of individual site design lends the ability to emphasize the bigger picture. The design process shifts to give more emphasis to where and why a building or site needs to be designed, a landscape enhanced, a street calmed, or a garden planted. This is the urban planner's unique role in the urban design process.

Finally, the approach is proactive in the sense that problem areas and design needs are first sought out and discovered, and then addressed. Often in urban design, the designer comes to the table with a site already predetermined. In these exercises, the discovery of where design interventions are most needed is a fundamental part of the design process.

Using this design approach, the following five principles underlie the form and content of each exercise:

1. Sustainability
2. Incrementalism
3. Social context
4. Policy and program
5. The world in layers

SUSTAINABILITY

There are many different ideas about how to connect urban design to sustainability. The book *Sustainable Urbanism* (Farr, 2007), for example, discusses how sustainability is increased through neighborhood stormwater methods, local food production, and district energy systems. Urban design can be used to protect habitat, maintain watersheds, and support all kinds of ecological systems through proper land development techniques.

The notion of sustainability used in these exercises is broad and doesn't really deal with things like green buildings and ecological systems. Instead, the following sustainability concepts underlie all of the exercises in this book:

- Each exercise assumes that cities should be designed for diversity—a mix of people, uses, and functions.
- Each exercise assumes that cities should be scaled to the walking human body rather than to the fast-moving private vehicle.
- Each exercise is intended for places that already exist. In the parlance of urban planning, this is urban design for infill, not greenfields.

Note that the third concept above puts some limits on the range of solutions available to the urban designer. While it may be possible to conceptualize a stronger neighborhood boundary, an additional neighborhood public space, or the insertion of a pedestrian pathway, design solutions that fundamentally change the street configuration or redesign the block system to be more interconnected are not very realistic proposals. Those kinds of urban design strategies are really only applicable to the design of entirely new developments.

INCREMENTALISM

Because the exercises are geared to existing urban places, the urban design strategies presented in this book tend to be modest and incremental. Taking a cue from Jane Jacobs, the book is based on the view that "emphasis on bits and pieces is of the essence: this is what a city is, bits and pieces that supplement each other and support each other" (Jacobs, 1961, p. 390). This is the part of Jane Jacobs's classic 1961 text, *The Death and Life of Great American Cities*, that is most in sync with the approach of this book—the part about how planners ought to spend their time nudging and tweaking rather than demolishing and building anew—making small, strategically placed interventions.

Of course, urban design is often posited in monumental terms—designs for airports, shopping complexes, and reconceptualized downtowns. While there are appropriate times for big architecture, the power of small interventions should not be underestimated. The ability to engage a wider segment of society in the design of place—one small, attainable intervention at a time—is one reason to embrace the "bits and pieces" approach.

Incrementalism also affects how ideas can be implemented. The design strategies articulated through these exercises can be realized by making only small requests of governments or property owners. Implementation may rest on, for example, instituting small grant programs or modest tax incentives. Above all, an incremental approach is a bottom-up approach—small-scale interventions that are manageable and resident-generated.

SOCIAL CONTEXT

As argued above, the urban design strategies used here are guided by a clear understanding of social context. Urban design is used to bridge the gap that often exists between social data and built form. The approach assumes that social need and economic justification must be viewed simultaneously. This is not always the case. The economic rationale almost always dominates where there is an intense interest in determining whether the proposed design strategy will give a sufficient return on investment. Less discussed is the idea that urban design should be undertaken to respond to the needs of the community as a social and communal entity.

This book relies on the idea that urban design is an important part of creating a more vibrant, sustainable, and socially just community. At the same time, these goals are not viewed as conflicting with the goal of creating more economic value. In fact, urban design can be used to help reduce potential conflicts between social and economic objectives by showing how similar the translations to built form can be.

POLICY AND PROGRAM

Urban design does not happen as something separate from policy and program. In fact, policies and programs have a profound impact on whether urban design interventions are successful. For example, if the urban design proposal is concerned with creating a neighborhood center, the policies required to make that happen—changing restrictions on use, redirecting capital investment, and providing incentives for property owners—will be as essential as the physical design itself. Policies and programs open or constrict the range of possibilities involved, narrowing the design alternatives. There should be no illusions: It would be impossible to implement the design strategies articulated in this book without giving adequate attention to policy and program.

Policies and programs are needed not only to implement design solutions but to help balance the negative economic and social costs that can unintentionally result from design intervention—especially displacement. A few examples include:

- Strategies to keep units affordable (community land trusts, inclusionary housing requirements);
- Strategies to entice the development of affordable units (tax credits, bonus densities);
- Strategies to preserve neighborhood assets (transfer of development rights, reuse of vacant and tax-foreclosed real estate);
- Strategies to retain rental units (condominium conversion ordinances);
- Strategies to keep buildings occupied (limits on the use of restrictive covenants);
- Strategies to revitalize the public realm (tax increment financing, loans, grants, bond financing, tax abatement); and
- Strategies to distribute tax dollars to the places that most need it (tax-base sharing).

Although these policies and programs are not covered in this book, their importance to the success of urban design should always be kept in mind.

THE WORLD IN LAYERS

Finally, because urban designers should be trained in the art of presenting alternatives, each exercise emphasizes the importance of articulating more than one design proposal for any given issue. This is approached mainly by structuring the analysis in terms of layers. Design alternatives are generated by turning layers on and off.

Urban designers should be especially adept at communicating design alternatives and making explicit what the options and what the consequences of those options are. It is also important to weave these alternatives into the design process, something to which a layered, exploratory approach is especially geared. With some control over the ability to turn layers on and off, anyone involved in the design process can have an impact on the range of possibilities presented.

STRUCTURE

This book is structured into 10 exercises covering 10 subject areas essential to community-based urban design. The exercises are grouped into three categories:

1. Exercises that have to do with the overall pattern of things;
2. Exercises that have to do with the basic elements of good neighborhood form; and
3. Exercises that cover the recurrent, special problems of urban design.

Each exercise covers an important aspect of the built environment that deserves special attention by urban planners.

The exercises combine methods (drawing, geographic information systems (GIS), Google SketchUp, image manipulation) that are typically divided between urban planning and the design professions (architecture and landscape architecture). The approach is strongly geographic, making use of spatial layers and incorporating locational analysis through GIS. This is combined with other techniques, such as the low-tech art of sketching, intended to emphasize the importance of experiencing and recording place quality through direct observation.

WHY, WHERE, AND WHAT

Each exercise is organized into three parts: background, analysis, and design. These correspond to "why," "where," and "what."

The background provides the why part—why is the topic important in urban design? To answer this, each exercise begins with a few key writings and a quick summary about the topic; for example, ideas about the ways in which the notion of "neighborhood" has been conceptualized, or a summary of why surface parking lots are considered in many cases to be detrimental to neighborhoods.

The analysis section is the where part of the analysis. Steps are laid out for uncovering all information necessary for the design phase. Where are there problems to be addressed and what criteria should be used to make that determination? Where should design interventions go, and where would they have the most impact? The analysis part begins with deciding what information is needed to fully understand a particular design problem, and then determining how that information could best be analyzed in order to narrow the range of locations.

Finally, in the design section of each exercise, a series of steps are presented for arriving at a set of design alternatives. This is the what part. Having established why an improvement is being suggested and where that improvement would be best located, it is then possible to decide what specific design alternatives can be proposed. What interventions in a given location make the most sense?

Together, these three parts—the background (why), the analysis (where), and the design (what)—form the basic outline of each exercise. They constitute a process for bringing ideas to the table, to be used in an interactive, exploratory way. The proposals are not blueprints; they are a set of ideas to be debated. The exercises are meant to foster exploration of the design potential of every neighborhood. They are tools to be used in an urban design process that is incremental and participatory. The very act of working through each exercise and reacting to the design proposals generated is a means of elevating the importance of design.

DESIGN ELEMENTS

More needs to be said about the what part of the design process used in this book. Many of the exercises make use of what could be termed "design elements." Quite simply, these are the relatively small things that make neighborhoods livable (for example, street furniture, civic spaces, and infrastructure of various kinds) that combine to create well-designed places. These design elements can be bigger (like squares, greens, and plazas) or smaller (like benches and crosswalks). They can be used to enliven, soften, connect, and strengthen, or they can be used to create focal points, vistas, and a sense of security.

Design elements are the building blocks used to improve the quality of neighborhoods. Of course, such elements cannot simply be plopped down here and there with the expectation that an improved place will result. That's why so much thought is given in each exercise to the why and the where part of the process that precedes the actual application of design elements. The key to successful urban design—the main approach used in this book—is to learn how to apply a given design element in a given place.

TABLE I-1

Design Elements*

Open space: plaza*, square*, green*, garden, small neighborhood park, large urban park, skate park, park with ballfield, park for recreation, dog park, playground, play lot*, pocket park*, multigenerational park*, greenway*

Retail: market district, market square, arcade*, atrium*, street market, open air market, cafe, food cart, news/magazine stand, kiosk*

Streets: crosswalk, sidewalk extension*, sidewalk and walkway paving, curb extension*, neckdown*, bulb-out*, chicane*, choker*, traffic circle*, roundabout*, bollard*, fences and separating walls, street trees, on-street parking (diagonal, head-in or -out, parallel), parking garage, parking sign/meter, shielded parking, bike lane and path, curb ramp, median*, diverter*, refuge island*, pedestrian signal, street painting/marking, transit stop and station, under- and overpass, bridge, alley, boulevard*, avenue*, multiway boulevard*, boulevard street*, woonerf*

Features: landmark, memorial, performance space and structure, flowerbed, planter, trees, tree fence, gazebo and shelter, gateway*, lighting, fountain and water feature, foot bridge, signage, shade structure, public art, mural, statue, tiles, chair, seat, bench, gate, wall, fence

*Elements with an asterisk are defined in the Glossary.

Design elements can be drawn from two main sources: (1) from books, web sources, and other published imagery; or (2) from personal experience. As a first step, a list of design elements should be generated by discovering the elements of urbanism that make for good places and making a record of them. This should be done at the start of the design process.

Listed in **Table I-1** are the primary categories of design elements often used in urban design. (Note: The Glossary gives definitions for some of the lesser known terms used in the Table.) Each category has literally hundreds of design possibilities, so this is obviously a representative rather than an exhaustive list.

Details on these design elements can be found in many publications, but here are a few useful sources:

- *Project for Public Spaces* (www.pps.org)
- Dan Burden, *Walkable Communities* (www.pedbikeimages.org)
- *Placemaking on a Budget: Improving Small Towns, Neighborhoods, and Downtowns Without Spending a Lot of Money* (Zelinka and Jackson, 2006)
- *SmartCode version 9 and Manual* (www.smartcodecentral.com) (Duany, Sorlien, and Wright, 2008)
- *The Great Neighborhood Book, A Do-It-Yourself Guide to Placemaking* (Walljasper, 2007)

Only a sample of the design elements listed in **Table I-1** are used in the exercises in this book. Often, only major categories are used; for example, "street upgrade" or "traffic calming," which could include a number of different ideas (such as crosswalks, street trees, benches, and decorative sidewalk paving). Very often, the point is not to engineer the exact details of a street improvement, but to suggest where the emphasis needs to go.

The design elements are applied in the exercises through the use of graphic symbols. Symbols communicate the desired interventions easily. The palette of symbols—and the corresponding intervention—is shown in **Figure I-2**.

Two other published sources relevant to these exercises should be mentioned. These are essentially encyclopedias of urban design strategies, which contain hundreds of pages of design elements drawn from around the globe and from all time periods.

The first is *The American Vitruvius: An Architects' Handbook of Civic Art* by Werner Hegemann and Elbert Peets, published in 1922. This is a classic text full of hundreds of beautiful illustrations (with 1,203 plates) of some of the best places and cities in the world (as of the 1920s). It includes plaza design, building ensembles, street design, and garden art. The second text is actually a follow-up to Hegemann and Peets's treatise, titled *New Civic Art: Elements of Town Planning*, by Andres Duany, Elizabeth Plater-Zyberk, and Robert Alminana. It builds on Hegemann and Peets's text to produce a more comprehensive atlas of design strategies.

FIGURE I-2

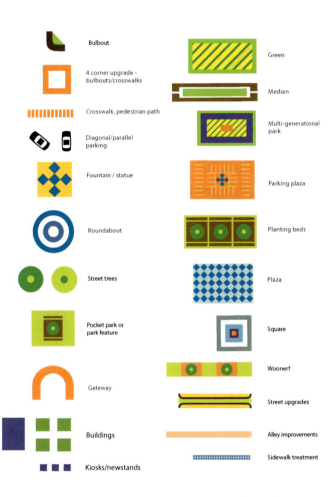

A list of symbols (representing design elements) can be used to easily map design strategies.

FIGURE I-3

FIGURE I-4

One conception neighborhood structure: Clarence Perry's famous diagram of the "neighborhood unit."

A second, perhaps more obvious, source of ideas is to simply find the elements, places, and urban conditions around town that are most appealing or inspiring, and photograph or sketch them. Anyone involved in the design process can create a visual list of desired design elements by just observing and recording the places, structures, blocks, buildings, gardens, and artwork around them. Places can also be found on the Internet and recorded by taking a screenshot.

The act of constructing a list of desirable design elements is valuable not only for the purpose of creating a resource list but also as a means of exploration. Every urban designer will tell you that experiencing a site by walking through it, observing it closely, photographing it, and sketching it—recording qualities that stand out or spark interest—is an indispensable method in urban design.

Every exercise in this book makes this assumption, and many of them include one or more steps that incorporate an experiential level of investigation. Sometimes this entails suggestions for experiencing key places by making sketches. **Figures I-3** and **I-4** are examples of the kind of simple sketches that could be useful. (The sketches are of places in the Portage Park area of Chicago—the case study used in this book.)

7

Building Types

Urban design often involves adding new buildings. Urban designers may want to suggest, in general terms, what types of buildings should be developed. The SmartCode is a good source for information on generalized building types (www.smartcodecentral.com). The SmartCode is an alternative type of zoning code based on different levels of urban intensity. In Table 9 of the SmartCode, "Building Disposition," four very general types are identified:

1. Edgeyard (single-family house);
2. Sideyard (duplex, zero lot line house);
3. Rearyard (town house, row house, apartment house, flex building, commercial block); and
4. Courtyard (patio house).

A more conventional approach to building typology is found in Understanding Architecture by Marco Bussagli. The following classifications are used in the chapter "Buildings and typologies": Habitations, Religious Buildings, Public Buildings, Military Construction, Towers, Skyscrapers and Lighthouses, Collective Architecture, Manufacturing Facilities, Service Facilities, Transportation Infrastructures, Commercial Buildings, Tombs and Cemeteries.

Other sources to consider are:

- *Ordering Space: Types in Architecture and Design*, edited by Karen A. Franck and Lynda H. Schneekloth;
- "Typology" by David Vanderburgh, in Encyclopedia of 20th-Century Architecture, vol. 3; and
- "Typology—an architecture of limits" by Doug Kelbaugh, in Architectural Theory Review.

The exercises in this book rely on three types of software: (1) GIS (mapping/spatial analysis); **(2) SketchUp** (3-D modeling); and **(3) Adobe Illustrator and Photoshop** (graphics). These products have become very user-friendly in recent years, and tutorials can get you up and running in little time. In addition to the tutorials that come with the software, there are some on-line resources that are especially useful.

Mapping/Spacial Analysis: GIS

The exercises require knowledge of only a few basic GIS operations: loading and overlaying map layers or "shapefiles," computing distance calculations to determine proximities, and selecting locations (parcels, buildings, and neighborhoods) based on certain criteria. There are different software products from which to choose, and open source GIS (free software) is widely available (http://opensourcegis.org or www.qgis.org).

ESRI, of course, is the industry standard when it comes to GIS and mapping software (their motto: "Better Decisions through Modeling and Mapping Our World"). In addition to the excellent tutorials that come with their ArcView software, you can learn GIS on-line. See ESRI's "virtual campus" (www.gis.com/education/online.html) for more information.

3-D Modeling: SketchUp

The exercises in this book also make use of SketchUp, a modeling software that allows you to show buildings and entire blocks in three dimensions. Viewing a street or even a whole neighborhood from the perspective of a low-flying airplane (an "axonometric" view) is now a relatively easy thing to accomplish. This is especially useful for analyzing changes in height and density, compatibility of infill development, sense of enclosure, and the effect of varying setbacks.

SketchUp is owned by Google, which makes it easy to place the 3-D models you create directly onto a map in Google Earth. You can also download complete building designs and other features from the "3D Warehouse" (http://sketchup.google.com/3dwarehouse) and place them directly into your SketchUp model. The free on-line training videos are excellent and are available at http://sketchup.google.com/training/videos.html.

Graphics: Adobe Illustrator and Photoshop

Graphics software—specifically Adobe Illustrator and Photoshop—are used in the exercises to apply symbols, color, imagery, and text to maps.

- Adobe Illustrator is a vector-based drawing program, which means it is especially good at drawing all kinds of lines and shapes.
- Photoshop is a raster-based graphics system, which means it is especially good at manipulation of digital imagery (represented as pixels).
- The two types of tools complement each other well.
- Like GIS and SketchUp, these tools come with excellent tutorials, but there are additional on-line resources to use. Here are two suggestions:
- Illustrator: www.indesign-studio.com/resources/tutorials
- Photoshop: www.webdesignerwall.com/tutorials

SOFTWARE AND DATA

The exercises make use of three kinds of software:

1. Graphical packages like the Adobe Suite of tools;
2. GIS software (ArcGIS), which allows spatial analysis in addition to graphical manipulation; and
3. Google SketchUp, which is a three-dimensional modeling tool.

The exercises assume only a very basic knowledge of the software. For each software tool, one can get to the required level of competence in only a couple of hours, assuming one is familiar with basic computer skills like how to use a mouse and open files and windows. Note, too, that each of these tools comes with tutorials designed to get the novice up and running in very little time. The sidebar gives more information on how to get started with the software.

Each exercise is structured in such a way that more than one tool is used. This is important because mixing tools and experimenting with their integration encourages innovative ways of observing, analyzing, and designing. Each type of software can be used to express design ideas, and each has pros and cons for doing so. SketchUp is great at 3-D representation, but 2-D graphics are difficult. GIS is great at 2-D and, beyond spatial analysis, graphic components can be added to include design ideas; however, 3-D modeling in GIS, while possible, is not as graphically adept as SketchUp. The Adobe products—especially Photoshop, InDesign, and Illustrator—are great drawing and illustration tools. Of course, any GIS or SketchUp output can be exported into drawing and illustration software to increase the quality of graphic output.

Although these exercises can conceivably be completed without these software tools, users will make the most effective use of these exercises if they have a basic working knowledge of these three types of software. Most important is an elementary knowledge of ArcGIS and SketchUp, followed by knowledge of Photoshop and Illustrator (see sidebar).

The three types of software—GIS, SketchUp, and Illustrator/Photoshop—are used for distinct, yet very basic, purposes. These can be summarized as follows:

GIS
- To see one layer of mapped data relative to other layers
- To determine what is nearby or within a certain distance of something
- To select a set of locations or elements based on certain criteria

SketchUp
- To show groups of blocks and buildings in three dimensions, especially from an axonometric view (low-flying airplane)

Illustrator/Photoshop
- To apply graphic symbols and text to maps. Although Adobe Illustrator is the graphics drawing system most often used, Photoshop is the preferred choice whenever digital imagery is imported into a map.

There are a few basic data requirements for these exercises such as land use by parcel, building footprints and heights, block outlines, street width, and some sociodemographic information. Aerial imagery is also important. Ideally, all of these layers will be available as GIS data. Note that data are referred to as "layers" because one set of data is overlayed with another—just like Ian McHarg did with transparent sheets of plastic in Design with Nature.

Any area of interest could be used for these exercises. One could simply select a group of census tracts (the most common spatial unit) or census block groups (a smaller spatial unit). Perhaps a cluster of 10-15 census tracts makes the most sense, in terms of having a wide enough array of material to analyze and design.

TABLE I-2

Selected Census 2000 Statistics for the Portage Park Community Area

Population	65,340
Population per square mile	16,417
% White	69.5
% Hispanic, 1990	7.8
% Hispanic, 2000	23.0
% Black or African American	0.51
% Asian	3.78
% 15 or younger	22.4
% 65 or older	18.4
Median household income	$ 45,117

Census tracts and census block groups are often used as proxies for neighborhoods because they provide an easy way to get a wide variety of socioeconomic data. Bear in mind that social scientists often use census tracts to define the boundaries of neighborhoods, and this is not completely arbitrary. Tract boundaries were initially defined by local committees of data users, using physical features and knowledge of the social and economic landscape.

THE CASE STUDY

All of the design exercises in this book use the Portage Park community area in northwest Chicago as the case study site. The use of an inner-ring suburb was preferred. Also called "first-tier" suburbs, these neighborhoods tend to have significant needs, and urban design is one of them. Recent studies have highlighted their development stresses—gentrification and displacement in some parts, but also a significant level of disinvestment and neglect (see Orfield and Puentes, 2002; Hudnut, 2003). There has been significant deterioration of these older suburbs in terms of infrastructure and basic services, but, at the same time, their populations are growing due to the arrival of recent immigrants. This adds up to a lot of potential for urban design intervention.

Portage Park has a familiar story. It started in the late 19th century as a commuter rail suburb. It was later absorbed by the City of Chicago, and now has a population of just over 65,000 (2000 Census). Its ethnic past was Polish, but, as in other inner-ring suburban areas in Chicago, the Hispanic population has been growing rapidly in the past two decades. Portage Park has a wide variety of uses, including industrial, major commercial, and public transit, in addition to many schools, parks, and local institutions. There is a wide variety of housing types and building ages. Portage Park is one of the most socially diverse parts of the city in terms of income, ethnicity, age, and family type.

An essential first step for these exercises is to construct a demographic profile of the area. This can be done using widely available demographic information found on websites like www.census.gov, www.socialexplorer.com, www.epodunk.com, or www.trulia.com. **Table I-2** lists a few key socioeconomic variables for the Portage Park community.

Figure I-5 shows the location of Portage Park relative to downtown Chicago (the "Loop"), as well as its population density relative to the rest of Chicago. The map indicates that this is a relatively dense community—a good example of a diverse, older urban neighborhood.

FIGURE I-5

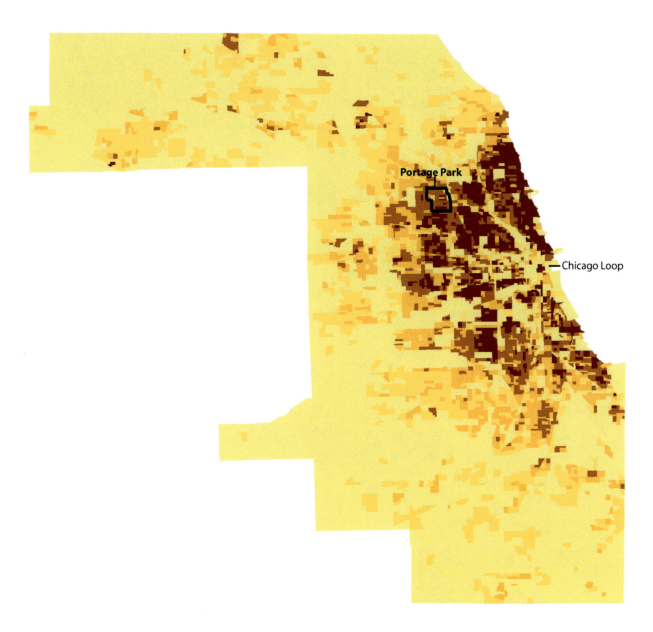

A list of symbols (representing design elements) can be used to easily map design strategies.

Seattle, Washington.
Credit: Abigail Keenan

GROUP 1
THE BIGGER PICTURE

Citywide issues requiring a big picture view Urban design can be approached at different scales. There are large-scale design issues involving entire regions, but there are also small-scale design issues involving single urban spaces. The important point is that urban design issues range from the more general to the more specific, depending on spatial scale, and that zooming in and out of an area determines the range of design elements that can be applied. Some design issues, such as connectivity, are relevant at any scale.

There are certain issues in urban design that are especially important to consider at a broader range and with a wider view—beyond a specific location, a segment of street, or an individual block or building. Such design issues involve a "big picture" view. This first group of exercises is devoted to design strategies that operate at this larger scale.

- **NEIGHBORHOODS**: Neighborhoods, variously defined, are the building blocks of the urban pattern.

- **TRANSECTS**: A transect considers patterns of urban intensity, ranging from rural to urban.

- **CONNECTIONS**: Connecting across multiple realms is essential.

Istanbul, Turkey.
Credit: Luke Michael

EXERCISE 1
NEIGHBORHOODS

***Purpose:** To delineate a set of neighborhoods for a given area*

BACKGROUND

Neighborhoods are tricky things. People have trouble defining what they are, especially from a social perspective. The point is often made that the definition of "neighborhood" is in the eye of the beholder, since there are so many varied interpretations of what "neighborhood" means. Some believe that spatially defined neighborhoods are unrealistic and irrelevant in any case, since people are not constrained to one particular area.

However, for the urban designer, the neighborhood is the basic spatial unit of an urban area. Even if people do, in fact, conduct their lives far afield, what happens within local contexts is meaningful. Establishing an overall neighborhood structure is important to urban design because it helps determine priority areas (for example, establishing where centers are most needed or most in need of support, based on how neighborhoods are spatially configured).

Most often, neighborhood structure is based on the walking distance between where people live and the goods and services they need on a daily basis, usually an area with a quarter- to one-mile radius (see discussion under "Size/Shape," below). There are many advantages to designing in function of walking distance. For example, many believe that walkable neighborhoods are necessary for creating locally based identity, increased social connectedness, a shared civic culture, and even physical health.

A close-knit neighborhood is believed to facilitate local governance and greater control over local planning issues. More practically, pedestrian-oriented neighborhoods are known to increase walking and therefore reduce dependence on the automobile. Within the neighborhood, daily life needs of all kinds—at least potentially—can be satisfied.

When urban design is organized around the idea of the walkable neighborhood, there are certain principles of form that come into play. In design terms, the ideal neighborhood most often includes:

- A center, where public and local institutional buildings are located (government administrative offices, community facilities, and other types of meeting places)
- Edges, which are meant to provide definition and connection, not exclusion
- A mixture of housing types designed to help ensure social diversity
- A mixture of functions, especially a school, parks, and local shopping
- A hierarchy of streets separating local and through traffic, but also providing connection across edges

Figures 1-1, 1-2, and **1-3** show three normative views about neighborhood structure. Clarence Perry's neighborhood unit, shown in **Figure 1-1**, is the most famous.

From an urban design point of view, the concept of neighborhood has generally varied along three dimensions:

1. Size/shape;
2. Function; and
3. Morphology

SIZE/SHAPE

Size implies both area (acreage) as well as distance and shape: whether there is a center or an edge, and whether the neighborhood is structured as a circle, square, or polygon. Neighborhood size is often defined by a circle with either a quarter- or half-mile radius from center to edge. Alternatively, size may be based on a square unit of 160 acres, or a quarter "section," derived from the Public Lands Survey, which laid out a substantial portion of the U.S. on a grid in the late 18th century. Neighborhoods can be as small as 40 acres.

These dimensions vary with location, density, and the type of "edges" that provide a logical boundary to the neighborhood. Edges may vary in character or type, either human-made or natural. In towns, recreational areas, greenways, schoolyards, and golf courses may separate neighborhoods. In very high-density areas, a neighborhood edge can be defined by rail lines and high-traffic streets.

FUNCTION

Function has to do with the activities and land uses within the neighborhood. Ideally, the neighborhood is mixed in use, including uses and facilities that serve the everyday life of neighborhood residents: shops, schools, and various types of institutions that serve a local clientele. In addition, neighborhoods are often conceived as containing a variety of housing choices, especially affordable housing options like garage apartments and other accessory units, apartment buildings adjacent to shopping, or apartments above shops.

The location of these functions is also critical. Neighborhoods can reserve priority locations for public space, civic buildings, or commercial uses. Centers can either be at the actual geographic center of the neighborhood or at the edge, along a major arterial. Plazas and squares, of varying sizes, may be dispersed to create special places throughout the neighborhood, or they can be consolidated in one location to create special districts. Public buildings may occupy important sites at the terminuses of streets. More regional, large-scale uses may be located at the edge rather than the center.

FIGURE 1-1

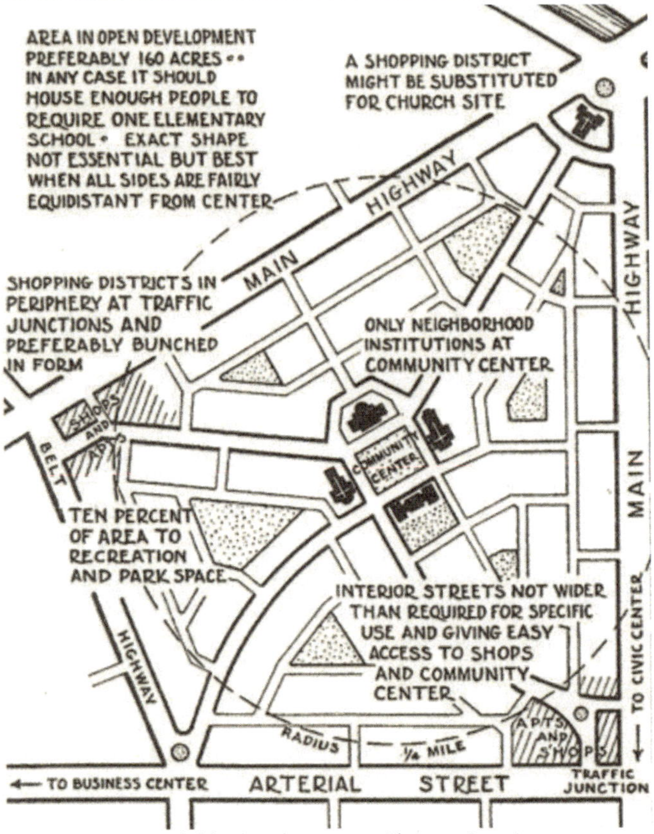

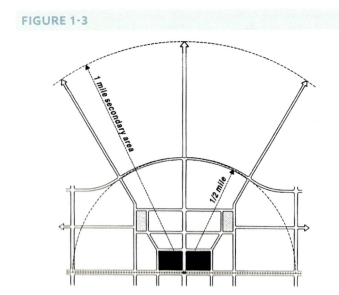

One conception neighborhood structure: Clarence Perry's famous diagram of the "neighborhood unit."

FIGURE 1-2

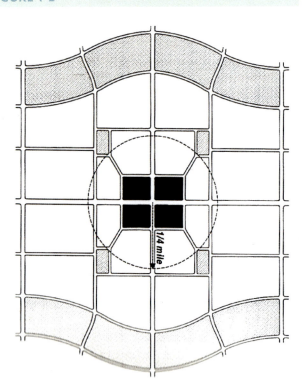

Alternative neighborhood diagrams: the livable neighborhood (left) and the transit-oriented neighborhood (left).
Source: The Lexicon of the New Urbanism.

FIGURE 1-3

MORPHOLOGY

"Morphology" refers to the pattern of streets, blocks, lots, and buildings. Such patterns can have a significant effect on neighborhood quality, character, and functionality. Especially important to the safe and efficient functioning of neighborhoods is the configuration of streets. Street layout not only creates block configurations for building sites but also affects traffic circulation. One particularly important consideration is whether local traffic is to be kept off regional roads or whether through traffic is to be kept off local streets. One theory is that an interconnecting pattern of streets provides multiple routes that diffuse traffic and lessen congestion in the neighborhood.

The morphology of traditional neighborhoods (pre-World War II) contrasts with post-World War II suburban development largely on the basis of street configurations (see Southworth and Ben-Joseph, 2003). One problem often cited is that the pattern of streets in newer residential areas tends to funnel traffic directly onto collector streets that connect at single points along major arterials. This makes street crossing hazardous and is indicative of a development pattern that favors the needs of cars over the needs of pedestrians.

Besides street patterns, block types with different dimensions and relationships to open space formulate neighborhoods of different kinds. Some argue that it is desirable to blend more than one block type in one neighborhood because this generates variety. Different block types have different implications for lot size and regularity (for example, whether lots have a particular size or shape consistency, or whether blocks can accommodate alleys). Smaller, more varied blocks and lots are often more successfully located toward the neighborhood center.

ANALYSIS

The goal of this exercise is to delineate the spatial boundaries of a set of neighborhoods within a given area. Each neighborhood within this overall framework will have a spatial delineation (size, shape) and a center. The overall task is to design a neighborhood framework—a set of neighborhoods determined by combining varying layers of information. Because different residents will have different views about the locations and boundaries of neighborhoods, it is important to propose more than one configuration.

Step 1: As a starting point, find out how well the neighborhood is currently "covered," based on preliminary assumptions about center locations.

Typically, central places—street intersections, civic spaces like schools and parks, and commercial areas—are used to construct a series of "pedestrian sheds"—the five-minute or quarter-mile walk around the central place. Assuming that all major intersections and public spaces are viable as neighborhood centers, **Figure 1-4** shows how well Portage Park is "covered." Almost everyone in the area has a center to which they can walk. Of course, as one digs a little deeper, it is easy to see that not all major intersections are likely to function well as neighborhood centers. **Figure 1-5** is one example, showing an intersection with weak delineation and therefore dubious value as a cohesive "center," at least in its existing form.

Step 2: Construct layers of information to be used in the delineation of neighborhood boundaries.

There are a number of variables to be considered when determining how to delineate a set of neighborhoods. To some degree, this will be determined by what data are available. Relevant data could be political, social, economic, or even cultural. Land use and characteristics of neighborhood form could also be used.

Start with political/demographic variables. Four variables are used in the examples below:

FIGURE 1-4

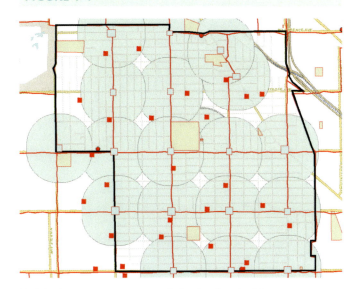

An initial assessment: quarter-mile "pedestrian sheds" cover most of Portage Park.

FIGURE 1-5

Not all major intersections can be expected to function as neighborhood centers. This one, for example, is weakly defined.

The map in **Figure 1-6** shows neighborhood boundaries as determined by the City of Chicago. Many cities have neighborhood maps just like this one. As indicated here, Portage Park is traversed by six different neighborhood boundaries. These neighborhoods were defined by planners working for the city, presumably using information collected from local residents. Historical boundaries like these could factor into the design of an overall neighborhood structure.

There are 12 census tracts covering the Portage Park community area, shown in **Figure 1-7**. Their boundaries are delineated by major streets. Assess whether there is any value in delineating neighborhoods coincident with census tracts, given that:

- They are logically bounded by major thoroughfares;
- These divisions might have made sense at one time, when tracts were first being delineated; and
- It would be easy to keep tabs on the sociodemographic changes taking place in these areas.

Police precincts are another way areas are socially delineated (see **Figure 1-8**). The boundaries of these precincts define police beats, and thus the spatial organization here is based on methods of community surveillance.

The map in **Figure 1-9** shows two layers: population density by block group and commercial parcels. Darker shades have higher density. There is some correspondence between commercial parcels and population density. Would these areas be the most appropriate nodes for neighborhood centers?

The map in **Figure 1-10** shows commercial areas (in red) together with aerial images of potential "edges" (in this context, places not easily traversed). These areas were identified through close inspection of aerial photographs. The areas not in white appear to be "blockages"—that is, large public, commercial, and industrial properties; large parcels of vacant land; major transportation corridors; or parks that most likely prohibit easy through-passage. How do these edges or blockages affect neighborhood structure? Should they be incorporated in neighborhood delineation, or serve as boundaries that define their spatial extent?

There are more traditional variables that could be used to delineate neighborhoods. Start by identifying known "central places"—significant commercial nodes, civic/public space, or intersections that could be conceived as neighborhood centers (places around which the neighborhood could coalesce, find its identity, and strengthen its civic and institutional base). The central places for Portage Park are shown in **Figure 1-11**, and essentially consist of public places like parks and schools, along with major intersections.

FIGURE 1-6

The officially designated neighborhoods of Portage Park. Source: The City of Chicago.

FIGURE 1-7

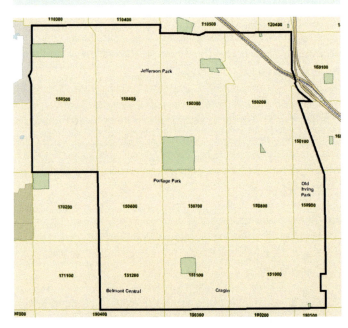

Census tracts are sometimes used as proxies for neighborhoods. Source: Census 2000.

FIGURE 1-8

Police precincts in Portage Park.

FIGURE 1-9

Population density and commercial land are other factors to consider in delineating neighborhoods.

FIGURE 1-10

Areas that are not whited out are potential neighborhood edges. Commercial uses are shown in red.

FIGURE 1-11

Traditional central places: parks, schools, and major institutions.

FIGURE 1-12

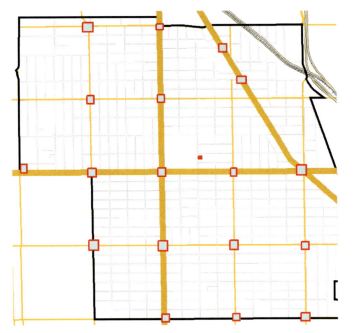

The hierarchy of streets in Portage Park: thicker lines have heavier traffic institutions.

FIGURE 1-13

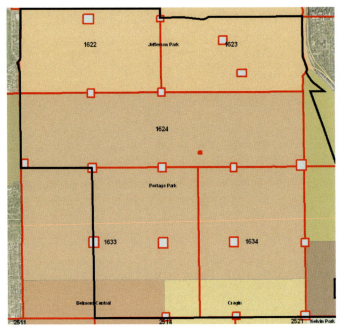

A combination of layers: centers, neighborhoods, and precincts.

FIGURE 1-14

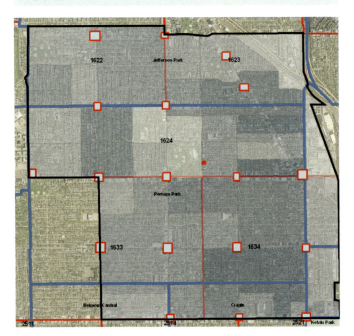

Another combination: centers, neighborhoods, and density.

FIGURE 1-15

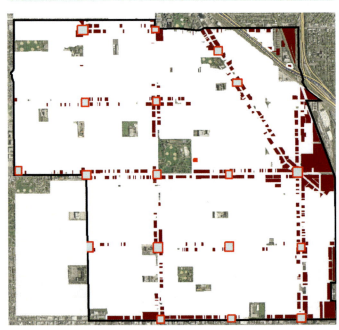

Another combination: centers, commercial areas, and edges.

FIGURE 1-16

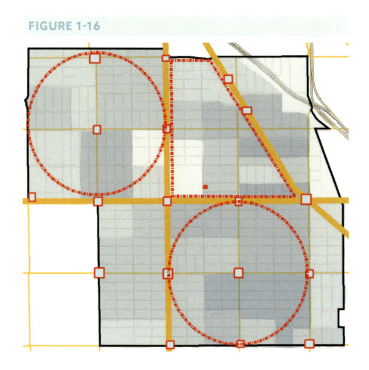

One possible set of neighborhoods.

FIGURE 1-17

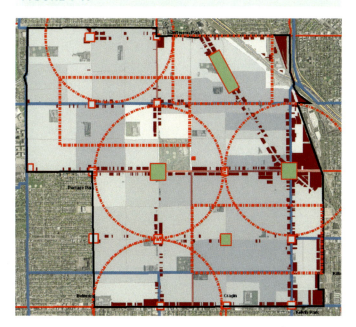

Another possible set of neighborhoods.

Finally, major thoroughfares could be used to define either a center or an edge of a neighborhood, and **Figure 1-12** shows the hierarchical street arrangement in Portage Park (as indicated by three different line thicknesses).

DESIGN

Step 3: With the layers of information obtained in Step 2, create one or more proposed sets of neighborhoods—a framework—to cover the entire community.

Rather than constructing a uniform coverage of quarter-mile pedestrian sheds, think about creating neighborhoods of different sizes in response to edges, the strength of centers, the location of thoroughfares, commercial spaces, and political and demographic information obtained in the first two steps—population density, police precincts, census tracts, and existing neighborhood delineation. For reference, neighborhoods are often sized at the following intervals:

- 40 acres (usually seen as a minimum; a quarter-mile square)
- 125 acres (a quarter-mile pedestrian shed)
- 160 acres (a half-mile square)
- 500 acres (a half-mile pedestrian shed)
- Shapes can also be irregular.

To begin the delineation process, try combining different layers and thinking about the relationships and their implications. For example, the following three figures combine neighborhood centers with:

- Administratively defined neighborhoods and precincts **(Figure 1-13)**;
- Administratively defined neighborhoods and population density **(Figure 1-14)**; and
- Commercial areas and edges **(Figure 1-15)**.

Figures 1-16 and **1-17** show two possible proposals for neighborhood delineation. There may be fewer centers proposed **(Figure 1-16)**, in which existing heavily traveled thoroughfares are used to delineate neighborhood boundaries. Alternatively, there may be different sizes and shapes of neighborhoods based on the strength and function of each center. **Figure 1-17** shows a rectangular neighborhood shape around linear centers (street sections), and a quarter-mile pedestrian shed around small institutions and neighborhood-level retail. A larger radius could be used around regional uses (high schools, regional shopping and offices) or located at the junction of several quarter-mile pedestrian sheds. Rail transit stops are also centers commanding a larger geographic catchment area.

More Questions to Ask

Neighborhood delineation is a very creative process. There are many questions to be posed, and the range of possible answers yields new layers of information useful for delineating an overall neighborhood framework. Here are a few examples:

- What centers are most important? Consider proposing neighborhood centers in areas currently underserved, especially areas of high population density. It may be a good idea to increase the size of an existing center to make it more "gravitational" (that is, serviceable to a larger geographic area).

- It may be useful to position centers adjacent to public spaces—especially parks—to create priority areas that can increase in strength and support a larger neighborhood size. Such centers may or may not be located at the geographic center of the neighborhood.

- Would the Portage Park community as a whole be better served by certain types of neighborhoods and centers as opposed to others (for example, schools, parks, commercial areas, or intersections as centers)? Is the area well covered by one type and not another?

- Identify where major thoroughfares are not actually functioning as edges or centers. Propose edges or centers at selected locations along major thoroughfares to help convert them to places with civic value.

- Determine the strength of each existing center. Sometimes a center is strong on one characteristic and weak on another. It might be possible to identify strengths and weaknesses that are appropriate to a given place. Is a commercially strong center appropriate in a place with lower population density? Is a place with high population density in need of a center, whose strength is that it is located at a major intersection?

- Are there situations where it might be useful to try to pull together two neighborhoods, in which case a strong center between them would be useful, or is the center meant to service a small, well-defined area?

- Does the neighborhood have more than one center? Perhaps there are two smaller centers linked by a commercial corridor. There may be two centers that are close together, in which case the center, and shape of the neighborhood, may be elongated.

- It may be valuable to keep a neighborhood within an existing administratively defined neighborhood. Alternatively, where there is a need to join larger, weakly formed neighborhoods together, propose strengthening centers that are centrally located and capable of serving that function.

- It may be useful to structure neighborhoods so that they respect police precincts, thus taking advantage of the existing spatial dimensions of the cop's beat. This may have value in trying to organize the neighborhood and institute neighborhood management strategies.

- Should neighborhoods be bounded by major arterials? Perhaps it makes more sense to keep neighborhood identity within major arterials. In other cases, however, it might make sense to attempt to link the areas on either side with a strong neighborhood center along the arterial. This is especially true where a major arterial cuts through an administratively defined neighborhood, a police precinct, or a tract with a meaningful delineation.

Cognitive Delineation of Neighborhood

A very different way of delineating neighborhoods could be accomplished by polling individual residents about how they define their neighborhoods. The notion of "cognitive mapping," a technique initiated by psychologist Edward Tolman in the mid-20th century, has been applied by many planners, notably Kevin Lynch.

The delineation of neighborhood in this approach emphasizes the fact that individuals have their own ideas about what constitutes their neighborhood. Many have argued that this fact—the individual nature of neighborhood definition and meaning—renders blueprint notions of neighborhood somewhat irrelevant. On the other hand, individual cognitive maps could be aggregated to produce an additional layer of neighborhood information.

A suburban community meets agricultural land in Ehningen, Germany.
Credit: Max Boettinger

EXERCISE 2
TRANSECTS

Purpose: To design a new zoning map based on the idea of an urban-to-rural transect

BACKGROUND

The design of a neighborhood is dramatically affected by zoning codes. Planners, who are generally the ones most associated with zoning and its administration, could exert a great deal of effect over the design of place by suggesting ways to overhaul existing, conventional zoning codes that tend to ignore their effect on design. Through innovative concepts like the urban-to-rural transect, which can be used as a basis for zoning, planners can have a major impact on design.

The "transect" is an analytical method that organizes the elements of urbanism—building, lot, land use, street, and all of the other physical aspects of the human habitat—in ways that preserve the integrity of different types of urban and rural environments (see Duany, Sorlien, and Wright, 2008). These environments vary along a continuum that ranges from less intensity (rural) to high intensity (urban). Adhering to this system of organization, each type of environment—whether urban, rural, or somewhere in between—is zoned in an effort to strengthen its particular character. The mixing of elements—a rural element in an urban environment and vice versa—is avoided.

Finding the proper integration of town (or city) and country (or nature) is a compelling subject. While it is possible to view the "man-made world" as "natural," it is more likely to be viewed in striking contrast to the natural world. The transect offers a way to find the correct balance. It ties into a tradition of ecological planning that is more integrative than boundary-driven. Rather than stopping urban growth with physical barriers that underscore urban versus rural division, the transect seeks to connect and integrate the two realms along a continuum. Thus, the transect can be thought of as an environmentally conceived approach to urban design.

The transects approach to the integration of urban and rural is an update on the idea of regionally dispersed garden cities. The modification accommodates a more diverse range of development types, paying greater attention to the interconnections of various urban elements at multiple points along the urban-to-rural gradient. This has the benefit of accommodating a greater range of development choices, infusing a greater sense of realism in the land development process. It also focuses on the need to work through existing development patterns. Rather than placing garden cities in a region, the transect seeks to position a more complex pattern of development types (known as "immersive" environments) in a regional framework. What is retained, however, is a clear focus on making sure that the integration of urban and rural places does not neutralize either one in the process.

This is appealing because it provides a basis for specifying a range of human habitats—habitats that can be coded much like conventional zoning, but with a much different purpose and approach. In recent years, attempts have been made to operationalize the transect idea by adapting it to an actual code. Duany, Plater-Zyberk and Co.'s SmartCode is the best example. It is a coding system based on the transect that identifies six zones or levels of intensity:

1. Rural preserve (T1)
2. Rural reserve (T2)
3. Sub-urban (T3)
4. Urban general (T4)
5. Urban center (T5)
6. Urban core (T6)

A category called "special district" applies to large facilities like airports and college campuses. **Figures 2-1** and **2-2** list and illustrate the characteristics of each zone.

Every city and town has its own set of urban-to-rural environments. Some of these environments are immersive in that the elements within them conform to a given level of intensity. Other areas are mixtures of different levels of urban intensity (for example, a skyscraper sitting in a cornfield is an urban element in a rural context, something the transect discourages). This exercise demonstrates how the various elements of the built environment fit together (or don't). It also shows how elements as basic as street widths and porch fronts can be used to code the character of a place. From visual inspection and mapped data, the ultimate goal is to derive a new zoning map based on the transect.

Some of the methodology used in this exercise is adapted from SmartCode version 9 and Manual (Duany, Sorlien, and Wright, 2008). Duany, Plater-Zyberk & Co. should be credited with the idea of applying the synoptic survey (a standard approach used in environmental analysis) to the human habitat. Further information about the transect and the SmartCode are available at http://smartcodecentral.com.

Note: This exercise uses four transect zones—T3 to T6—to show the complete range of transect zone variation as proposed in the SmartCode. It should be kept in mind, however, that this is a long-term, future-oriented perspective, as it is unlikely that Portage Park will contain true "urban core" conditions in the near term.

FIGURE 2-1

| T1 NATURAL ZONE | T2 RURAL ZONE | T3 SUB-URBAN ZONE | T4 GENERAL URBAN ZONE | T5 URBAN CENTER ZONE | T6 URBAN CORE ZONE | SD SPECIAL DISTRICT |

Transect zones: from rural to urban.

FIGURE 2-2

T3 — T-3 SUB-URBAN
T-3 Sub-Urban Zone consists of low density residential areas, adjacent to higher zones that some mixed use. Home occupations and outbuildings are allowed. Planting is naturalistic and setbacks are relatively deep. Blocks may be large and the roads irregular to accommodate natural conditions.

- **General Character:** Lawns, and landscaped yards surrounding detached single-family houses; pedestrians occasionally
- **Building Placement:** Large and variable front and side yard Setbacks
- **Frontage Types:** Porches, fences, naturalistic tree planting
- **Typical Building Height:** 1- to 2-Story with some 3-Story
- **Type of Civic Space:** Parks, Greenways

T4 — T-4 GENERAL URBAN
T-4 General Urban Zone consists of a mixed use but primarily residential urban fabric. It may have a wide range of building types: single, sideyard, and rowhouses. Setbacks and landscaping are variable. Streets with curbs and sidewalks define medium-sized blocks.

- **General Character:** Mix of Houses, Townhouses & small Apartment buildings, with scattered Commercial activity; balance between landscape and buildings; presence of pedestrians
- **Building Placement:** Shallow to medium front and side yard Setbacks
- **Frontage Types:** Porches, fences, Dooryards
- **Typical Building Height:** 2- to 3-Story with a few taller Mixed Use buildings
- **Type of Civic Space:** Squares, Greens

T5 — T-5 URBAN CENTER
T-5 Urban Center Zone consists of higher density mixed use building that accommodate etail, offices, rowhouses and apartments. It has a tight network of streets, with wide sidewalks, steady street tree planting and buildings set close to the sidewalks.

- **General Character:** Shops mixed with Townhouses, larger Apartment houses, Offices, workplace, and Civic buildings; predominantly attached buildings; trees within the public right-of-way; substantial pedestrian activit
- **Building Placement:** Shallow Setbacks or none; buildings oriented to street defining a street wall
- **Frontage Types:** Stoops, Shopfronts, Galleries
- **Typical Building Height:** 3- to 5-Story with some variation
- **Type of Civic Space:** Parks, Plazas and Squares, median landscaping

T6 — T-6 URBAN CORE
T-6 Urban Core Zone consists of the highest density and height, with the greatest variety of uses, and civic buildings of regional importance. It may have larger blocks; streets have steady street tree planting and buildings are set close to wide sidewalks. Typically only large towns and cities have an Urban Core Zone.

- **General Character:** Medium to high-Density Mixed Use buildings, entertainment, Civic and cultural uses. Attached buildings forming a continuous street wall; trees within the public right-of-way; highest pedestrian and transit activity
- **Building Placement:** Shallow Setbacks or none; buildings oriented to street, defining a street wall
- **Frontage Types:** Stoops, Dooryards, Forecourts, Shopfronts, Galleries, and Arcades
- **Typical Building Height:** 4-plus Story with a few shorter buildings
- **Type of Civic Space:** Parks, Plazas and Squares; median landscaping

Each transect zone has a different set of specifications regarding form and use.

The Synoptic Survey

The synoptic survey is typically used for environmental analysis to determine the characteristics of a given site by discovering the habitats (or "communities") that it contains. The objective is to determine the values of each habitat in order to recommend the degree of protection and type of restoration each might require. Every functioning habitat is a symbiotic community of microclimate, minerals, humidity, flora, and fauna.

In environmental analysis, the synoptic survey is a systematic visual inspection that identifies typical habitats: a wetland here, an oak hammock there, a rocky outcrop there. The most representative locales are then analyzed in depth by means of the dissect and the quadrat. The "dissect" is a simultaneous analysis of the conditions above and below ground, and involves borings to determine such items as the soil condition, water table, and archeology.

FIGURE 2-3

QUADRAT

DISSECT

Quadrat analysis involves counting elements within a given area. Dissect analysis entails taking a slice through the environment and measuring its characteristics.

The "quadrat" involves taking a normative area (say, 100 x 100 feet) where the component elements of flora and fauna are itemized and counted.

The concepts and methods that are used to analyze natural habitats—the synoptic survey, the transect, the dissect, and the quadrat—can be extended into urbanized areas. **Figure 2-3** shows some example dissect analyses for urban and natural environments.

From SmartCode version 9 and Manual (Duany, Sorlien, and Wright, 2008), available at http://smartcodecentral.com.

ANALYSIS

Step 1: To get a baseline, carefully examine the existing zoning map of the area.

The Chicago zoning map for Portage Park is shown in **Figure 2-4**. Note the many different zones, as well as their diverse sizes and shapes. There are many categories, each with its own set of rules for permitted use, densities, setback requirements, and other standards (www.cityofchicago.org/zoning). Portage Park has 28 separate zoning categories. The transect approach to zoning greatly simplifies this complexity, using only four categories of built environment (and two others for natural, unbuilt lands).

Step 2: Examine existing areas in terms of their transect qualities.

Most urban, built-up areas the size of Portage Park will already have a range of existing transect zones, although the zones are not likely to be highly immersive in every case (where every element conforms to its location along the transect). To get a sense of this, examine the main dimensions and elements in each of four transect zones that are likely to exist, including both the elements on private lots and within the public right-of-way. Record the key elements that conform to the generic descriptions of each transect zone shown in **Table 2-1**. When taken together, the list of elements for each zone shown in Table 2-1 gives a good clue about the transect zone variation that exists in Portage Park.

Step 3: Construct the layers that will be used to determine transect zone locations.

To delineate transect zones, one approach is to use blocks as the unit of analysis and assign a particular transect character to each block. In the example below, three criteria are used:

7. Major streets and the blocks adjacent to them;
8. Density by block; and
9. Land-use intensity.

Figures 2-5, 2-6, and **2-7** show these three layers for Portage Park. **Figure 2-5** shows the blocks that fall into two categories: blocks that are adjacent to a major street or boulevard in Portage Park, and blocks that are not. **Figure 2-6** shows blocks that have been assigned a certain density level. Densities were determined based on census data at the block-group level. Based on the range of densities found in Portage Park, blocks were put into one of five density categories.

Figure 2-7, constituting land-use intensity, was determined using parcel data from the county tax assessor. One of four use categories was assigned to each parcel:

10. Single-family detached dwelling;
11. Residential apartment building, row house, or town house;
12. Mixed commercial/residential; or
13. Nonresidential (commercial or industrial).

Next, each block was assigned a level of land-use intensity based on the make-up of parcel-based land use for the block. Specifically, the following criteria were use:

- Level 1: Single-family dwellings constitute 50 percent or more of the parcels on the block.
- Level 2: Single-family dwellings constitute less than 50 percent; in addition, there are residential apartment buildings, row houses and town houses on the same block.
- Level 3: The percentage of parcels that are row houses, town houses, or apartment buildings is greater than the median percentage for the area (in this case, greater than 23 percent).
- Level 4: The percentage of mixed commercial/residential, commercial, or industrial parcels exceeds 30.5 percent, comprising the top 40 percent of all blocks.

The three layers used here account for much, but not all, of transect zone variation. Other layers that could be used include:

- Private frontage (categorized by parcel)
- Public frontage (categorized by parcel)
- Open space categorization

These could be constructed as additional layers, where each parcel or block is assigned a value, and layers are then combined to derive the boundaries of each zone. Determining these values by block would most likely involve a combination of fieldwork and close aerial map inspection.

DESIGN

Step 4: Create a new zoning map based on transect categories.

Design intervention for this exercise consists of first producing a new zoning map, and then characterizing each of the zones in more detail. As noted above, the transect zoning map will be much simpler and have far fewer zones than the existing zoning map.

The final transect zoning map, shown in **Figure 2-8**, is a combination of the three layers derived in Step 3. Specifically, using residential density (units per acre), street type, and land-use intensity, **Table 2-2** shows the combination of values for the layers that was used to assign each block to a transect zone category. For example, if a block was not on a major street, was in the lower 60 percent in terms of density, and had a land-use intensity of "Level 1" (single-family dwellings constituting 50 percent or more of the parcels on the block), then the block would be assigned a transect zone of T3.

Figure 2-10 is a three-dimensional view of one section of Portage Park, showing transect zone categories in relation to building density and form. It indicates a high level of intensity around the park (T5), where there are some apartment buildings, while the highest level of intensity (T6) is reserved for the blocks along the main commercial corridor. The intensity level becomes higher as the commercial section becomes more pronounced (toward the right-hand side of the graphic). Other blocks lessen in intensity as they move away from the park and the commercial corridor.

Using the transect zones derived by overlaying these layers of information, fine-tune the boundaries of transect zones by looking more closely at the aerial maps and visiting selected areas as needed.

Step 5: Select four representative areas to examine in depth.

Use the map **(Figure 2-8)** to select representative areas for the four built-up zones of the transect (T3, T4, T5, and T6). Visit the four areas selected and make a visual inspection. Verify that the areas are generally representative of the four transect zones; if not, consider fine tuning the map and selecting new representative areas.

At this point, if an actual code were to be calibrated, it would be necessary to take more detailed measurements of urban elements and characteristics. This would start with a recording of the urban dissect (a cross section) and then the urban quadrat (average measures) of each zone. For the dissect, the SmartCode recommends recording a cross section of the public realm (streets, sidewalks) and the private realm (frontages, buildings). The elements are photographed and sketched in cross section, and measurements are taken by using a tape measure or by counting steps. If unknown, building height can be approximated by measuring the length of a shadow of something with a known height (a person, for example), and applying the same ratio to the shadow of a building.

For the quadrat, the SmartCode recommends taking a four-acre area and recording the collective ratios or average measures for lot coverage (average size of buildings divided by average size of lots), average lot width, average lot length, number of parking spaces (on-street versus off-street), number of dwellings (units per acre), number of accessory units, and length of block perimeter.

TABLE 2-1

Transect Zone Descriptions for Portage Park*

	T3	T4	T5	T6
Land uses and buildings	Houses	Houses, town houses, limited commercial	Town houses, apartments, hotels, office buildings	High- and mediumrise apartments, office buildings, hotels
Private frontage	Lawns, porches, fences	Porches, fences	Stoops, shopfronts	Stoops, forecourts, shopfronts
Public frontage	Open swales, naturalistic tree planting	Raised curbs, narrow sidewalks	Raised curbs, wide sidewalks	Raised curbs, wide sidewalks
Thoroughfares	Roads	Streets, rear lanes	Boulevards, avenues, streets	Boulevards, avenues, streets
Open spaces	Parks, greens	Squares, playgrounds	Squares, plazas, playgrounds	Squares, plazas, playgrounds

*Adapted from the generic description of each transect zone found in the SmartCode; includes elements most relevant to the Portage Park community.

FIGURE 2-4

There are 28 Zoning categories in Portage Park.

29

Step 6: Calibrate the transect zones.

The SmartCode provides a starting table (Table 14 in the SmartCode), which gives generalized, generic parameters for each transect zone. In a full-blown recoding effort, everything recorded in the quadrat and dissect measuring steps would be entered into this table, wherever appropriate.

A simplified version is shown in **Table 2-3**, which offers a description of each transect category in Portage Park. It was filled in by taking averages for characteristic zones.

If needed, it would also be useful to add district boundaries (for example, for hospitals, campuses, museum complexes, and industrial parks) as well as T1 preserve (protected land) and T2 reserve (future protected land) boundaries.

Note that transect zone delineation also involves a process of identifying areas that are in nonconformance with the new transect zones (for example, blocks that exceed the maximum targeted perimeter, densities that are too low, or lot widths that are too wide). Those areas can be identified as "transitional," constituting places where the new transect zoning rules will allow them to evolve according to transect intensity and character rather than land use (as is conventionally the case). According to the theory of the transect, designing for this kind of evolution—based more on urban form than prescriptions about use and floor area ratio—will produce a more complex and satisfying urbanism.

FIGURE 2-5

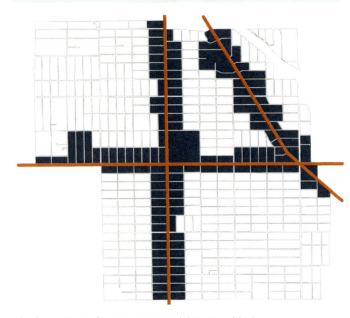

The first criterion for transect zone delineation: blocks near major thoroughfares.

FIGURE 2-6

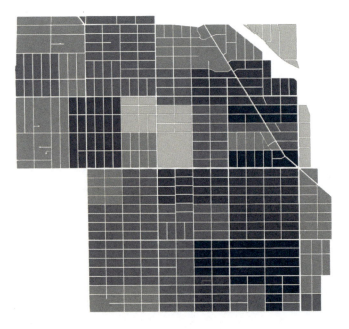

The second criterion: population density by block (darker=denser).

TABLE 2-2

Rules for Transect Zone Assignment

	T3	T4	T5	T6
Street type	Not on major street or boulevard	Not on major street or boulevard	May or may not be on major street or boulevard	On major street or boulevard
Density	In lower 60% of density	In lower 60% of density	In lower 80% of density	In upper 20% of density
Land-use intensity	Level 1	Level 2 or Level 1 and T-zone < > 3	Level 3	Level 3 or 4

FIGURE 2-7

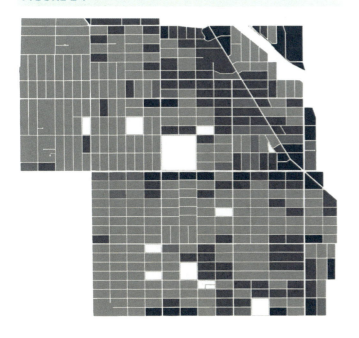

The third criterion: existing land-use intensity (darker=denser).

FIGURE 2-8

Proposed transect zones for Portage Park.

FIGURE 2-9

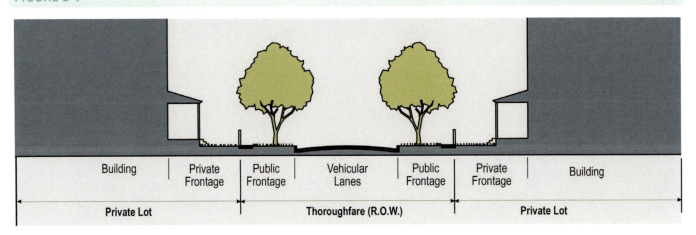

Public versus private frontage. Source: SmartCode.

FIGURE 2-10

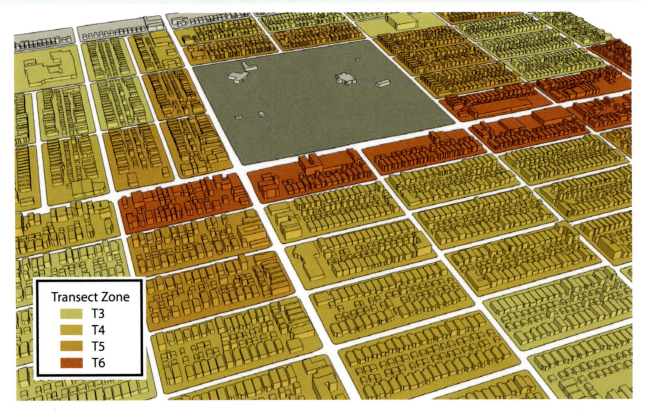

Transect zones and building form.

TABLE 2-3

Local Calibration of Transect Zone Characteristics

	T3	T4	T5	T6
Base residential density (units per acre gross)	4 units per acre gross	6 units per acre gross	8 units per acre gross	12 units per acre gross
Block size (max. block perimeter)	3,000 ft. max.	2,000 ft. max.	2,000 ft. max.	2,000 ft. max.
Thoroughfares required, permitted, or not permitted	Commercial street not permitted	Roads* not permitted; alleys required	Roads not permitted; alleys required	Roads not permitted; alleys required
Civic spaces required, permitted, or not permitted	Plazas not permitted	All permitted	All permitted	Greens not permitted
Lot width	30 ft. min., 100 ft. max.	18 ft. min., 100 ft. max.	18 ft. min., 100 ft. max.	18 ft. min., 100 ft. max.
Lot coverage	60% max.	70% max.	80% max.	90% max.
Front setback (max.)	14 ft. min.	18 ft. max.	12 ft. max.	12 ft. max.
Edgeyard building permitted/not permitted	Permitted	Permitted	Not permitted	Not permitted
Sideyard building permitted/not permitted	Not permitted	Permitted	Permitted	Not permitted
Building configuration (max. and min. no. of stories)	2 stories max.	3 stories max., 2 min.	5 stories max., 2 min.	8 stories max., 2 min.

* "Roads" are a specific category of thoroughfare appropriate in lower intensity, less urban environments.

The Ginza district, in Tokyo, Japan.
Credit: Redd Angelo

EXERCISE 3
CONNECTIONS

Purpose: *To identify places where connectivity could be improved, and then suggest strategies for improvement*

BACKGROUND

In urban design, connectivity is an essential theme (see especially Hillier and Hanson, 1984; Alexander, 1965; Salingaros, 1998). The idea has parallels to the notion that diversity is central to good urban neighborhoods, a tenet of urban design famously proffered by Jane Jacobs. Cities and neighborhoods that maximize mix and increase the connections between people and things are thought to be more vibrant and healthy. Strategies for increasing connectivity are based on the view that the built environment has an effect on constraining or promoting passive contact, an essential aspect of neighborhood-level social interaction (Fischer, 1982; Gehl, 1987). Interaction at this scale is a pedestrian phenomenon dependent on street networks and the social connections that happen as a result of them (Michaelson, 1977; Grannis, 2003).

Connections vary by scale, involving different types of routes. For example, urban designers may talk about regional connections in terms of highways and other major transportation routes, or about neighborhood-level connections via streets and greenways. Connections at smaller scales, such as by block or individual lot, will involve a discussion of even smaller types of routes and pathways. Connecting all types of spaces is important—public and private, residential and nonresidential, storefront and sidewalk.

Connection can involve a linear route or a central place. It can involve movement along a path or between two points, or it can focus on a central location that serves as a connecting space. In terms of the latter, it has already been argued that the establishment of neighborhood-scale central places has connective value. Neighborhood centers promote connectivity by providing a space of common identity, a public area to which residents might be drawn and become connected to one another within, simply by sharing the same space at the same time. Similarly, facilities like schools can be located in centralized places where they can maximize their ability to function as shared spaces that foster social connectedness. The provision of public spaces for casual or spontaneous interaction is not intended to create deep social bonds, but instead promotes "weak" social ties that are not only necessary and important but are believed to be especially sensitive to environmental design (Skjaeveland and Garling, 1997).

Routes, paths, or other corridors are often the means of connection. A common strategy for promoting connectivity is to ensure that streets are well connected. Streets have an obvious effect on separation and the disruption of neighborhoods. A recurring phenomenon in urban places is overly busy thoroughfares—streets with six lanes of traffic buzzing through the center of a residential area. Such roads have value as external connectors, but the cost is high: disruption of pedestrian quality and a lack of connectivity at a smaller scale.

A focus on street connections draws attention to the size and shape of blocks, which have a significant impact on the corresponding patterns of movement. It is generally agreed that large-scale blocks, cul-de-sacs, and dendritic (tree-like) street systems are less likely to provide good connectivity. The patterns in **Figure 3-1** from The Lexicon for the New Urbanism are examples of different block arrangements and corresponding street patterns, showing how connectivity is affected.

Note that, of these historical examples, a gridded street pattern is believed to offer the best connectivity because it provides multiple paths between points. This not only disperses traffic but also allows pedestrians to navigate the shortest possible distance between two points.

While the study of varying street patterns is informative, it does not provide much guidance in trying to come up with alternative design strategies for improving connectivity in established urban neighborhoods. This exercise is not concerned with proposing new street layouts; the intent is to improve connectivity in neighborhoods that are already built out, where street patterns cannot be changed.

The exercise focuses on connectivity via movement corridors of various types—from major thoroughfares to pedestrian paths—rather than attempting to enhance connections that occur within public spaces (since that aspect is treated elsewhere). The goal will be to find strategic areas where design interventions to improve connectivity will have the most effect. A crucial first step is to find places that are lacking connectivity, and then decide where blocked

FIGURE 3-1

Block arrangements and street patterns: square; elongated; irregular (2); Radburn; Riverside; Savannah; Washington, D.C.
Source: The Lexicon of the New Urbanism (Duany, Plater-Zyberk & Co., 1998)

FIGURE 3-2

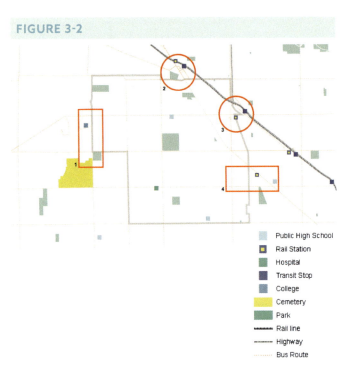

Clusters of regional facilities and routes.

FIGURE 3-3

"Hotspots" of connectivity problems.

areas need to be redesigned. Connection isn't necessarily to be enhanced at every location. In some cases, the lack of connection may be useful or even required.

ANALYSIS

The analysis involves looking at three scales of connection:

1. Regional-level connections, since neighborhoods benefit from being connected to the larger area or district of which they are a part;
2. Places that seem to have connectivity problems, by virtue of being sequestered or within enclaves; and
3. Connectivity patterns within the areas immediately surrounding neighborhood centers, since these areas would stand to gain the most by having good connectivity to the center.

Step 1: Find the regional systems—roads, greenways, transit lines—that intersect the neighborhood.

These include regional routes like bus and rail lines and major streets, rail stations, hospitals, colleges, high schools, large parks and cemeteries, farmers markets, and major employers. Identify the points at which the neighborhood connects to these regional systems.

Figure 3-2 shows five locations where there are clusters of regional facilities and routes.

Step 2: Identify areas likely to have connectivity problems.

Look closely at the following layers: streets, blocks, parcels, and land use. Identify areas that may have connection problems:

- Cul-de-sacs and dead-end streets
- Housing areas built after 1960
- Large blocks
- Multifamily housing arranged in "superblocks," constituting residential enclaves and sequestered housing that is shut off from the rest of the neighborhood
- Large parcels

Figure 3-3 shows six areas where the above layers overlap. These are, in a sense, potential "hotspots" of connectivity problems.

FIGURE 3-4

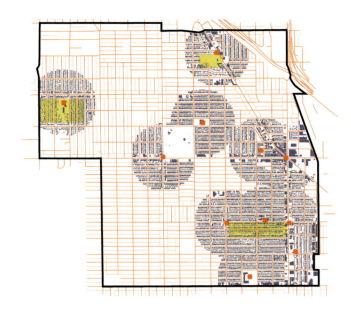

Yellow areas seem to have poor connectivity to their neighborhood centers.

FIGURE 3-5

Clusters of activity spaces: churches, schools, stores, and other community facilities.

Step 3: Using the neighborhood centers identified in the neighborhoods exercise (Exercise 1), delineate the five-minute walking radius around each and identify the routes they contain.

In Exercise 1, areas that could function as neighborhood centers were identified, based on a number of social and other criteria. In the areas around these potential centers, connectivity is especially important. How do residents from surrounding locations get to the center? Routes should include both streets and alleys.

Figure 3-4 identifies neighborhood centers and highlights areas (in yellow) that seem to have poor connectivity within the five-minute pedestrian shed surrounding them.

Step 4: Identify clusters of activity spaces (places that should have a high degree of interconnectivity).

Find the most important neighborhood focal points and highlight those that are relatively close together. For example, churches, schools, stores, and other public institutions and community facilities are places that would benefit from being well connected to one another. These form clusters of activity spaces, and should ideally be connected to form a mutually reinforcing network. Determine this by looking at the connecting routes within the clusters of neighborhood focal points.

The connections among neighborhood focal points become especially important because their connectedness can produce neighborhood synergies—something greater than the sum of their parts. In a sense, individual places increase their value through their connection to other places.

Figure 3-5 shows five areas where there are clusters of different kinds of activity spaces (commercial in blue, public and quasi-public in yellow).

Step 5: Examine in detail the routes within neighborhood center pedestrian sheds (Step 3) and within clusters of neighborhood focal points (Step 4).

Walk along the routes in the areas identified in Steps 3 and 4 and identify two kinds of blockages:

1. Direct blockages, which are physical barriers like dead-end streets and cul-de-sacs; and
2. Indirect blockages, such as empty spaces, vacant lots, and parking lots, which can disrupt pedestrian routes.

Also include areas with insufficient places to cross existing streets, and streets that disrupt connection by being too wide or too busy and are therefore hostile to pedestrians.

FIGURE 3-6

Design to improve regional connectivity: area 1.

FIGURE 3-7

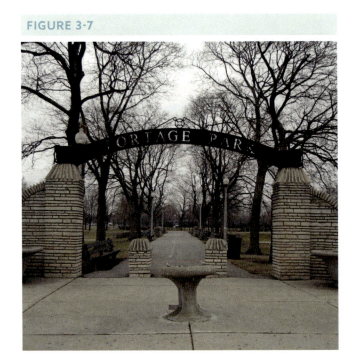

Gateway to Portage Park.

FIGURE 3-8

Design to improve regional connectivity: area 2.

DESIGN

There are a number of ways to improve connectivity within the high-priority areas identified above. Urban designers can recommend relatively small interventions to help improve connectedness (for example, by adding, extending, or improving pedestrian paths, midblock crossings, crosswalks, alleys, and bike paths).

Beyond finding the shortest path between two points, improving connectivity may involve emphasizing additional, alternative routes to bypass the busiest streets, or completing networks of greenways that are distinct (and separate) from automobile routes. It may involve ensuring that alleys are navigable, especially wherever streets don't provide a good route for pedestrians.

Step 6: Improve connections to regional systems.

Regional facilities draw from a wider area. For the areas identified as being important for regional connection in Step 1, suggest design strategies that build on this regional pull.

Figure 3-6 shows area 1 (from **Figure 3-3**) which has a variety of regional facilities, including a college campus, a cemetery, a park, major arterial roads that link the neighborhood of Portage Park to adjoining neighborhoods, and bus and bike routes. The figure identifies a corridor to be upgraded (point B) in order to support the regional anchors at either end. At point A, some kind of gateway could be placed in order to strengthen this location as an entrance (the entrance to the neighborhood is currently graced only with parking lots on three sides).

The small gateway represented here (perhaps an arch, similar to the one shown at the entrance to Portage Park, **Figure 3-7**) would span corner improvements that acknowledge the significance of this location as a regional entrance and connector. Similar corner treatment would be needed at the other end of the corridor, where a park currently sits. The corners opposite the park are now vacant or used for parking, underplaying the regional importance of this intersection.

Another regional connecting point (area 3 on **Figure 3-3**), shown on **Figure 3-8**, consists of two parks, a major highway, a rail line, bike paths, major streets, and a train station. There are several green, open spaces that seem only randomly placed. These regional facilities could better serve the neighborhood if they were designed to connect. **Figure 3-8** shows the train station and the parks on either side linked by a new pedestrian pathway. The pathway traverses parking lots and connects to the various green spaces. The station area has been improved to include a larger plaza or public space (point B) that joins the two pathways extending to either park. The pathway connecting the two existing parks is anchored on either end by a significant park feature (a group of benches, a fountain, or artwork).

A final design intervention motivated by regional elements is shown in **Figure 3-9**, showing area 3 on **Figure 3-3**. Again, this is an area with major transportation corridors and an existing park on one side. The strategy here is to improve the ability of pedestrians to traverse these regional systems, thus giving the corridor a connecting identity and function. This requires making upgrades at point A, and completing the connecting route at point C to the park.

Currently, the major street connecting either side of the highway/rail corridor is a virtual wasteland. Point A can be improved to function more like a gateway—shown here are crosswalk improvements and small infill buildings to give the corner more importance. At point B, there is a private facility (a tennis club) that could play a role in the proposed linkage as an additional stopping point—or at least a recognizable visual amenity—along the route.

Step 7: Improve connectivity in problem areas.

For the areas identified as having potential connection problems in Step 2, several strategies can be suggested. It is important to note that connection problems are more relevant when examining connections among places. In other words, "bad connectivity" is most relevant if one is trying to connect one place to another; otherwise, the idea of connectivity is something of an abstraction.

FIGURE 3-9

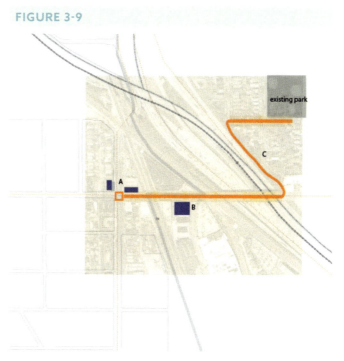

Design to improve regional connectivity: area 3.

FIGURE 3-10

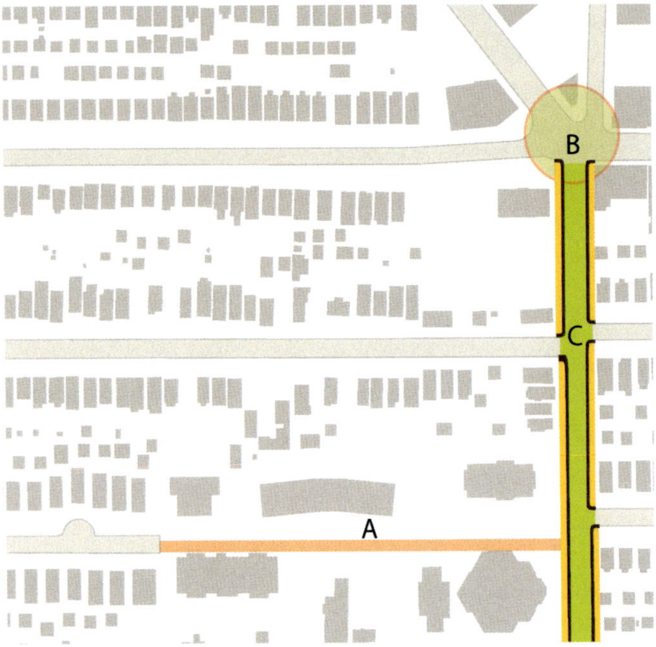

FIGURE 3-12

Design to improve connectivity in problem areas I: connecting the cul-de-sac.

Design to improve connectivity in problem areas III: a square enlivens small retail.

FIGURE 3-11

Design to improve connectivity in problem areas II: a multigenerational park connects two diverse housing areas.

FIGURE 3-13

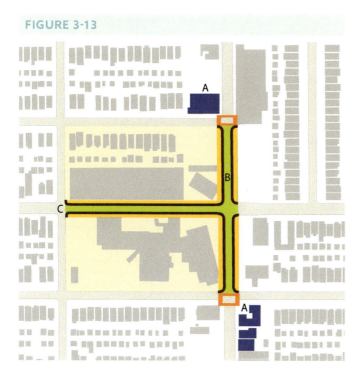

Design to improve connectivity in problem areas IV: breaking through a "clogged artery."

Figure 3-10 shows one of the areas identified as having more than one overlapping layer of connectivity problems. It shows a cul-de-sac and large blocks with large buildings. It is possible to improve connectivity by inserting a pedestrian pathway (point A) that connects the cul-de-sac to the street. This would make the most sense if there were a "gravitational pull" at point B, something to which the adjoining neighborhoods would want to connect. Also important would be to improve the corridor at point C, which is weakly defined with vacant lots and parking lots fronting the street. Corridor improvement could involve new trees, sidewalk extensions, upgraded sidewalks, and a variety of other pedestrian amenities and traffic-calming measures.

Figure 3-11 shows an area with new housing and relatively large blocks, signaling potential connectivity problems. Here, connectivity would be improved if there were a connecting point or location among the different housing types—new town houses and apartment buildings on one side, and older, single-family homes on the other. Shown here is the insertion of a multigenerational park among the housing types, which could provide an important connecting space.

Another area identified as potentially problematic in terms of connectivity is shown in **Figure 3-12**. This three-dimensional graphic illustrates that in this "sea" of bad connectivity—an edge area with large blocks, large buildings, and new condos organized as enclaves, all adjacent to a highway/rail and industrial corridor—there is an existing, smaller-scale building that houses neighborhood-serving retail. This small commercial space serves an essential role as a connector for the area. To sustain this commercial space as a viable neighborhood focal point with a connective function, a small square has been added adjacent to these buildings. There is also a need to make sure the routes leading to this cluster of buildings and square from all surrounding points are maintained or even enhanced (for example, with consistent sidewalk paving or landscaping), particularly as new development emerges in the area.

Finally, **Figure 3-13** shows a disruptive set of blocks—a hospital complex—situated in the heart of a neighborhood, between two dense residential areas. These blocks act like a clogged artery—blocking connection to either side. In this case, there are existing destinations drawing residents (for example, smaller retail establishments at point A to which residents could connect) To improve the connection, however, there should be street calming and intersection upgrades along routes B and C.

Step 8: Improve connectivity within walking distance of neighborhood centers.

To improve the connectivity of neighborhood centers, add pedestrian pathways and modest street and sidewalk improvements within the areas surrounding them. These improvements reinforce connection by creating visual and functional linkages. Connectivity can be improved by adding benches, painted or textured sidewalks, and street trees along the route. Crosswalks at all street crossings are also important. The idea is to focus improvements on the pathways that connect to neighborhood centers.

The example in **Figure 3-14** shows how alleys can be important for improving connectivity. Here, the school (a neighborhood center) fronts an alley on one side. By adding a square on this side and improvements to the alleys, the connectivity to the school is improved. If passage along the alley is viable, it reduces the physical (and perceptual) distance between the school and the surrounding residences. Crosswalks that link alleys are also essential. Two example alley treatments in residential areas are shown in **Figure 3-15**; alleys don't always have to be for garbage cans and garages.

Routes to neighborhood centers need to be deliberate and unambiguous. Look for ways to maintain the shortest paths, and determine whether it would be possible to cut pathways through lots at some locations. Instead of paths that fizzle and stop indeterminately, it would be useful to continue routes and paths in a deliberate and direct way, to break through blockages and make spaces more permeable. Parks should end with pathways rather than stopping abruptly.

FIGURE 3-14

Design to improve connectivity in problem areas IV: Improved connections to the center.

FIGURE 3-15

Alleys can make pleasant pedestrian pathways in residential areas.

FIGURE 3-16

Activity clusters I: strip mall activation.

FIGURE 3-17

Activity clusters II: improving a corridor with a strong cluster of active uses.

FIGURE 3-18

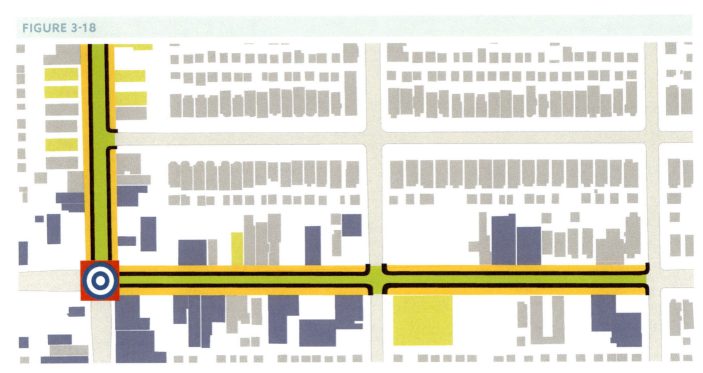

Activity clusters III: a pivotal point between two public realms.

FIGURE 3-19

Activity clusters IV: street upgrades around a church complex.

Step 9: Improve connections within activity clusters.

Finally, urban designers can propose interventions within areas that contain clusters of active uses—the blockages identified in Step 5. Where there are empty spaces that disrupt the ability of the street to function as a connector, there should be an emphasis on infilling empty spaces around these clusters, and adding buildings, plazas, parks, playgrounds, street trees, and other kinds of elements.

Small interventions can go a long way to enhance connectivity within clusters of supporting neighborhood uses. A related, regulatory approach would be to add a "build-to line" to help create a better sense of enclosure, especially on the street near clusters of activity. This would help the street maintain its function as an important part of the connective public realm.

Figures 3-16, 3-17, 3-18, and **3-19** all show clusters of active uses—commercial in blue, public and quasi-public in yellow—where the connectivity around, between, and among these uses and buildings could be improved.

Figure 3-16 proposes an activation of sidewalk space in front of an existing parking-fronted strip mall, perhaps with small-scale, outdoor retail spaces like magazine or produce stands. The space should be targeted because it is centrally located in the middle of many nonresidential, neighborhood-supporting functions.

Figure 3-17 shows an area where the street corridor runs the length of a high number of neighborhood-serving focal points. Because of this cluster of active uses, the corridor should be targeted for improvements like street trees, upgraded crosswalks, benches, and other amenities.

Figure 3-18 shows a pivotal point between two public realms—a group of publicly owned buildings to the north, and a public school to the east. In between are a number of commercial uses. The intersection should be strengthened as a way of pulling the two sides together. This could be accomplished by adding a traffic circle and crosswalks on all sides, and trying to make better use of the street corners (with the encouragement of infill development).

The final example, **Figure 3-19**, shows a street complex surrounded by retail uses occupying small buildings. Street identity via corridor improvements will connect the church complex (yellow buildings) to the surrounding cluster of nonresidential uses.

Manhattan, New York City.
Credit: Barron Roth.

GROUP 2
BASICS

Design to support the essential characteristics of a neighborhood.

The best designed neighborhoods have a few basic qualities in common. They often have a center and an edge(s), a mix of people and uses, and good access to goods and services (proximity). This group of exercises looks at these basic features in detail, stressing the importance of specific sites and their design.

The social geography of the neighborhood becomes especially important vis-à-vis the locational aspects of these features:

- **CENTERS**: What neighborhood centers should consist of, how they should function, and what should be around them are all important questions for urban designers.

- **EDGES**: Edges have multiple functions and can be made permeable.

- **MIX**: Design can play a role in supporting the mix of uses and the mix of people in a neighborhood.

- **PROXIMITY**: Design can help enhance proximities among people, goods, and services.

A Hong Kong market at night.
Credit: Samuel Chan

EXERCISE 4
CENTERS

Purpose: *To suggest design improvements that can be used to enhance neighborhood centers*

BACKGROUND

Neighborhood centers are "centers" in the sense that they provide a common, centrally located destination for surrounding residents. They are often thought of as being the actual geographic heart of a neighborhood, but that is not a strict requirement. However, if they can be positioned in a geographically central way—that is, in the center of a population—this is an efficient arrangement because it maximizes the number of people with access to them.

On a pragmatic level, centers provide needed services for people, ideally within walking distance. On social and civic levels, centers provide a means of connecting people—to one another, and to some larger common, public purpose. They are a physical articulation of "community"—a tangible, permanent symbol of the common bond that people living in the same neighborhood share. The neighborhood center provides a place for spontaneous interaction, which, potentially, fosters a sense of social connection. In addition, centers may, over time, promote a sense of shared responsibility.

It is difficult to have a neighborhood center function as a center if it is excessively large, like a baseball stadium or a high school surrounded by acres of open space. If large land uses make up what is generally regarded as the neighborhood's center, access to it may be low because of all the surrounding land area required. Lower walking access requires the addition of parking lots, which further increases the amount of land area needed. Large, publicly owned vacant parcels are therefore avoided as possible centers because they lack good accessibility and are usually positioned not as centers but as peripheral uses.

Centers should be valued spaces in the neighborhood. They can consist of any combination of land uses, but there is often some public component. The public space incorporated in a center—intended explicitly for public use and publicly owned—can be formally designed as a green, a plaza, a square, or other formal space. The SmartCode identifies five different types of civic spaces, and any one of these could function as an appropriate neighborhood center, or part of one, in the right context (shown in **Figure 4-1**).

Parks, clusters of commercial buildings, and other focal points and common destinations in a neighborhood can function as centers. Schools are a particularly interesting case. In the history of urban planning, there is a long tradition of trying to use schools as community centers. The school was part of the community center at the heart of Clarence Perry's 1929 neighborhood unit idea (shown in **Figure 1-1**). The U.S Department of Education made some effort to strengthen this tradition and issued a publication in 2000, called Schools as Centers of Community: A Citizens' Guide for Planning and Design, summarizing the benefits and laying out policy directives.

ANALYSIS

Step 1: Characterize the different kinds of centers already identified during the neighborhoods exercise (Exercise 1).

Those centers were identified as:
- Schools and school grounds
- Libraries
- Community centers or other publicly owned buildings
- Parks
- Intersections of main streets

Figure 4-2 shows the locations of these different types of centers. Visiting, sketching, and photographing potential centers are especially important for this exercise. Try to get a sense of whether each place is functioning like a center, or whether each

FIGURE 4-1

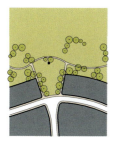 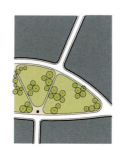 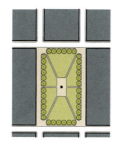  

Types of civic spaces: park, green, square, plaza, playground. Source: SmartCode version 9 and Manual (Duany, Sorlien and Wright, 2008).

FIGURE 4-2

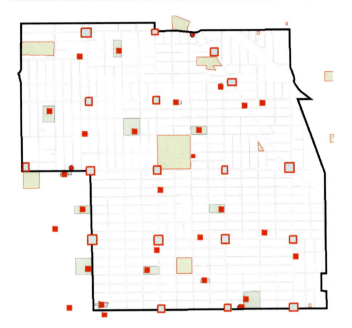

Different types of neighborhood centers in Portage Park.

FIGURE 4-3

Sketch of a neighborhood center in Portage Park. Sketch by Elif Tural.

FIGURE 4-4

Sketch of a neighborhood center in Portage Park. Sketch by Elif Tural.

could, given the right interventions. Also try to identify a local vernacular for the public and commercial spaces each contains. **Figures 4-3** and **4-4** are two example sketches of places that currently serve as neighborhood centers in Portage Park—a public park and a major retailer at a centrally located intersection.

Step 2: Identify types of centers based on additional layers of information.

The character, functionality, and design requirements of each of these centers will vary along different dimensions. The following dimensions could be used to characterize these differences more specifically:

- Who lives around and near them
- What their primary use is
- Their combination of uses
- Their physical condition
- Their degree of public access, and whether they include public land
- Their current ability to function adequately as centers

Take stock of these centers by creating layers of information and then combining these layers to specify different types of centers. For example, start with these layers:

- Schools
- School playgrounds
- Parks
- Major streets
- Busy intersections
- Population density
- Multifamily housing units
- Commercial (retail) areas
- Publicly owned land

Combine these layers in different ways to create different metrics for the idea of a "center." Combining layers of information in this way helps identify the kind of center for each location. Four examples are given below.

Schools as Centers

Combine the following layers:
- Schools
- School grounds
- Concentrations of multifamily housing

Select schools to be used as centers based on the relationship among these three layers. The results are shown in **Figure 4-5**.

The following criteria were used in the selection:
- The schools should be adjacent to school grounds of some kind so that a public space can be developed that does not require entry into the school building; and
- The school should be located near multifamily housing in order to maximize the number of people with walking access to it, and because multifamily housing has lower access to private outdoor space than single-family detached housing.

Parks as Centers

Combine the following layers:
- Parks
- Major thoroughfares

Select parks to be used as neighborhood centers based on the following criteria:
- The park has an unambiguous main entrance (or one could be created) that could serve as the focal point of the center; and
- To maximize exposure and increase utility of the area as a center, the main entrance should be situated on a major thoroughfare.

These two criteria create the subset of neighborhood centers shown in **Figure 4-6.**

Commercial Areas as Centers

Combine the following layers:
- Commercial land
- Major thoroughfares
- Areas with high population density

Select commercial areas to be used as neighborhood centers based on the following three criteria:

1. The center should be anchored by retail use;
2. It should be located along a major thoroughfare, to take advantage of its high exposure; and
3. It should be located near areas of high population density, to maximize pedestrian access.

These three criteria create the subset of neighborhood centers shown in **Figure 4-7**.

FIGURE 4-5

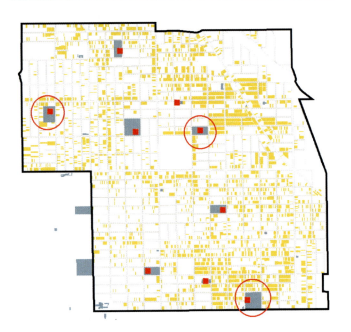

Schools as centers.

FIGURE 4-6

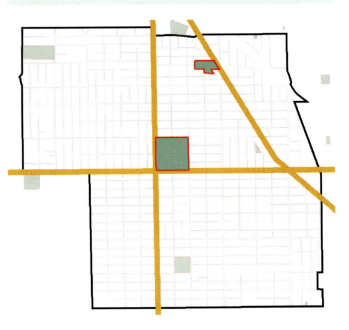

Parks as centers.

FIGURE 4-7

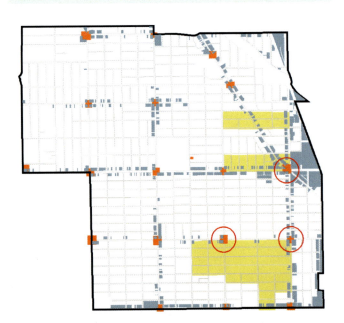

Commercial areas as centers. Yellow areas have the highest population density.

FIGURE 4-8

Publicly owned land where new centers could be created.

New Centers

Combine the following layers:
- Publicly owned or tax-exempt land, excluding parks and schools
- Areas with high population density

Select potential new centers based on the following three criteria:

- Land that is publicly owned, either vacant properties or vacant buildings;
- Clusters of publicly owned lots or buildings where there is enough space to transform the area into a neighborhood center; and
- Areas near high population density, in order to take advantage of pedestrian access.

These criteria create the subset of neighborhood centers shown in **Figure 4-8.**

Step 3: Visit and record observations about each type of center.

Visit one of each of the types of centers selected above. Take pictures and make sketches. During the visit, record observations about the following questions. The questions are adapted from the evaluation list developed by the Project for Public Spaces (www.pps.org):

- Within the space: What is the character and ambiance of the space? Are there places to sit comfortably? Does this space appear to function as a neighborhood center—is it well populated? What activities are observed? Are people of different ages present? Are people in groups or alone?
- The approach: Do streets around the space affect it positively or negatively? Are the surrounding streets too car-intensive or too car-dominated? Are there sidewalks going to the space and connecting it to surrounding areas? Do street intersections seem hostile to pedestrians, or can pedestrians easily get to the space?
- The enclosure: Is the space enclosed, or is it more open? Does the space "hang together" well as a center? What is the relationship between open space and building? Can the space be seen from across the street? Is it too enclosed? Does the openness or enclosure need to be addressed? Is the center surrounded by parking lots, undefined open space, or blank walls?

DESIGN

The analysis above resulted in the selection of four different kinds of centers. Each type of center was visited to better understand activity patterns, approach, and enclosure.

Design strategies can be proposed that recognize the fact that different kinds of centers will have different design needs. Some key things to consider—the results of which will vary by center type—include the following:

- Frontage: Is there good building frontage, for a sense of enclosure around the space, or are there weaknesses that need to be mitigated? Is there one side on which to focus, and others to leave as is? Should some frontages be lined or wrapped with more permeable, pedestrian-friendly frontage?
- Uses: Is there a good mix of uses at the center (especially public versus commercial)? Are there uses that should be added, such as facilities or commercial spaces, or even parking? Could existing uses like parking lots be given dual purpose?
- Entrances: Are there well-designed entrances and gateways to the center?
- Connections: How do people from all points around the center get to the center? Are the surrounding street crossings appropriate?
- Elements: What design elements might be added on the site to improve its function as a plaza, square, green, or other civic space?

Step 4: Propose design strategies for each type of center.
Schools as Centers

Figure 4-9 shows a design intervention to support the use of a school as a neighborhood center. The area around this school has the right ingredients: publicly owned land and high-density housing.

Several strategies could improve the status of this space as a neighborhood center. First, create a plaza where there is currently a parking lot (point A). A plaza is a paved (hardscaped) public space, usually fronted by civic or commercial buildings. There is a good opportunity here to create a plaza at point A, since this open space (now a parking lot) has a school on one side and multifamily residences on adjacent corners. Plazas can be created out of parking lots with minimal means. They can retain their function as parking lots during certain times of the day, but change into a functional civic space when parking is not needed. This is common in Europe, where plazas have long had a dual purpose (see **Figure 4-10**).

FIGURE 4-9

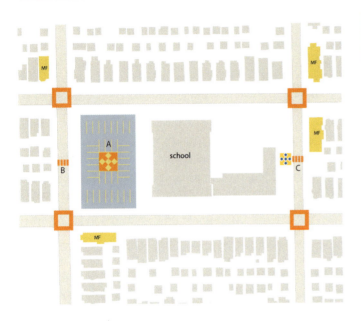

A school site as a neighborhood center. (MF=multifamily).

FIGURE 4-10

European plazas serve a dual purpose: parking areas that can also be used for civic functions. Source: New Civic Art.

FIGURE 4-11

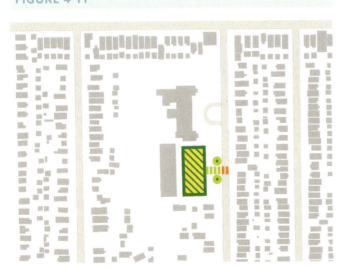

School site as a neighborhood center.

FIGURE 4-12

Parks as centers I: focus on the entrance.

Second, connections all around should be enhanced—at the four surrounding intersections, and where the alleys dead-end on school property on both sides (points B and C). There is also an opportunity at point C to install something more substantial, like a fountain, which would provide a less ambiguous entrance and connecting point to the neighborhood.

Figure 4-11 shows another example. The entrance of this school is already well designed. It emphasizes the civic importance of the school with a nicely landscaped circular drive; however, the open area below the school is an afterthought. It could be upgraded and more formally designed as a green in order to establish its role as a civic center for the neighborhood. Connecting the space in front of it by installing a midblock crossing could give added emphasis.

Parks as Centers

Portage Park, for which the community area is named, has a weak presence as a center. Surrounding its entrance are parking lots and car dealerships—signifying a lack of connection to the surrounding area, and little recognition that the park is the social and geographic heart of the community. **Figure 4-12** shows one design strategy. Incentivizing infill development on the parking lots across the street from the main entrance (point A) would help emphasize the importance of the park. Infill buildings here would give the main entrance some enclosure, putting more focus on the entrance by framing it. Better connections (crosswalks, bulbouts) at the intersection immediately adjacent to the park's entrance (point B) would support pedestrian access to it. Midblock crosswalks at points around the park would also help.

The park shown in **Figure 4-13** could serve as a center if the connections between the park and the surrounding area were more deliberate; better designed crosswalks and other pedestrian upgrades at key intersections would be an important start. The connection at intersection A could be especially important for drawing the northward neighborhood residents "in" to the center. At point B, there is a need for a focal point, a termination at the end of the vista (for example, as conceptualized in Figure 4-13, a fountain).

FIGURE 4-13

Parks as centers II: connections and focal points.

FIGURE 4-14

Commercial areas as centers: upgrade a parking lot surrounded by commerce.

FIGURE 4-15

European plazas serve a dual purpose: parking areas that can also be used for civic functions. Source: New Civic Art.

FIGURE 4-16

New centers: capitalize on a cluster of publicly owned buildings.

Commercial Areas as Centers

Figure 4-14 shows a possible neighborhood center tucked within a busy commercial area. The current use is a large parking lot that could be converted to a parking plaza, enlivened with new development (live/work units are shown), and provided with connecting crosswalks or other pedestrian upgrades. The space is slightly off the main thoroughfare but thoroughly embedded in a mixed use area that currently lacks a central focal point.

In the center of the plaza, there could be a small, central meeting spot, perhaps like the one shown in **Figure 4-15**. Better pedestrian treatment at the surrounding intersections could help draw residents from the adjacent blocks, and give a better sense of connectedness to the center. The terminated vista at point A in **Figure 4-14** could have a more interesting entrance treatment, signifying from a distance that the space has civic value, beyond car storage.

New Centers

The area shown in **Figure 4-16** is made up predominantly of publicly owned land and could be transformed to function as a neighborhood center. Using public buildings as anchors, the parking lots could be developed as dual-purpose plazas. The adjoining intersection could be upgraded with pedestrian-enhancing bulbouts, medians, and other intersection enhancements that signify the importance of this place as a neighborhood center.

Buenos Aires, Argentina.
Credit: Sander Crombach

EXERCISE 5
EDGES

Purpose: *To identify the edges in a neighborhood and propose design interventions that could mitigate their harmful effects*

BACKGROUND

"Edges" in urban neighborhoods can be defined as large urban elements that are either nonpermeable (acting as barricades and separators) or permeable (acting as seams). Typical examples are transportation corridors like highways and rail lines, large pieces of land like shopping malls and parking lots, or large industrial sites and vacant land. Where edges act as seams, they draw the places on either side together.

In neighborhood planning and design, edges and boundaries can be problematic concepts. Although the notion of an "edge" is a recurring criterion for the well-formed neighborhood because it gives it definition, it can also exclude and isolate. Edges are supposed to bound and give shape and identity (or legibility) and, ideally, they are supposed to function like seams and lines of connection rather than barriers. Where edges are composed of transportation corridors and industrial sites, however, they are most likely not functioning like buffers filtering a disturbance, but are themselves part of the "disturbance."

Edges formed by large transportation structures do not necessarily have to be detrimental to a neighborhood, but often urban infrastructure is not designed with neighborhoods in mind. It would be wonderful if every large piece of urban infrastructure were built with civic purpose, the way many public works projects were built in the early 20th century. The cloverleaf intersection shown in **Figure 5-1** from the Master Plan of Highways of the County of Los Angeles, California shows just how beautiful such projects could potentially be.

Fortunately, there are ways urban designers can address edges, besides offering complete redesigns for urban infrastructure. In keeping with the focus of this book, the designs proposed here will stick to more modest and feasible interventions that don't require huge sums of public money, but that do require some creative thinking.

Edges composed of functional space, like commercial areas, have a better chance of serving the function of seam rather than barrier. They may function as both streets for passing through a neighborhood as well as thoroughfares connecting residents on either side. Their linear structure promotes movement through the corridor as well as movement across.

Ecologists talk about edges and boundaries in a way that might have relevance to urban design (see especially Dramstad et al., 1997). Ecologists are particularly interested in edge structure (width and composition), the shape of boundaries (whether straight or not, for example), and what these characteristics mean for maintaining edge versus interior species. They consider the function of an edge—whether it is acting as a filter that buffers surrounding influences, and whether the edge is of sufficient width

FIGURE 5-1

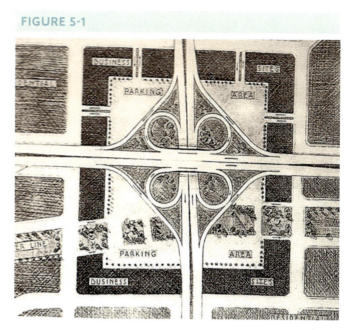

An artfully designed cloverleaf intersection, early 20th century. Source: Master Plan of Highways of the County of Los Angeles, California (Los Angeles County Regional Planning District, 1941).

to protect interior habitat from disturbances like wind and sun.

The abruptness of an edge influences whether movement occurs across the edge or alongside it. Similarly, boundaries that are straight will tend to generate movement along the boundary, whereas "convoluted" boundaries may encourage movement across boundaries. Boundaries can also be thought of as being "hard" or "soft." All of these ways of thinking about edges in ecological terms can be applied to the analysis of edges in urban areas.

ANALYSIS

The analysis of edges starts by first identifying where edges in a neighborhood are, and then classifying them according to one of three types. This is necessary in order to target design interventions appropriately.

Step 1: Find the main edges in the community.

Figure 5-2 shows the most obvious land uses that are used to identify urban edges: highways and transportation corridors, and industrial sites and brownfields. **Figure 5-3** adds another layer: large parcels (vacant parcels, clusters of vacant parcels, or large parks). **Figure 5-4** shows the composite: edge areas distributed throughout the Portage Park community.

FIGURE 5-2

Edges I: transportation corridors and industrial sites.

FIGURE 5-3

Edges II: large vacant parcels and large parks.

FIGURE 5-4

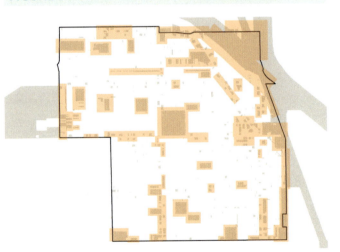

The main edges in Portage Park.

FIGURE 5-5

Internal edges can affect connectivity.

FIGURE 5-6

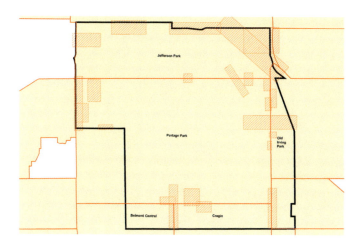

Edges and neighborhood boundaries.

FIGURE 5-7

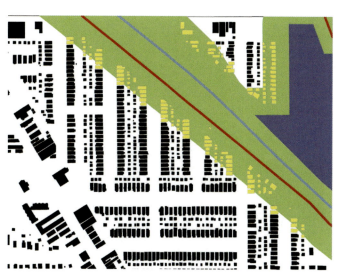

A strong edge (highway/rail) adjacent to incompatible uses (residences).

Step 2: Narrow down the selection of edges.

Since there are so many potential edges in a community, it is necessary to devise a way to narrow down the selection and focus on those edges that are most in need of addressing.

Many of the interior edges, such as those found in **Figure 5-5**, are a result of large parcels, functioning as a kind of internal edge. These can be set aside for now, as they were the focus of intervention in the connections exercise (Exercise 3).

Instead, focus on those edges that coincide with neighborhood boundaries. **Figure 5-6** shows the locations of the neighborhood boundaries running through Portage Park, together with those edge areas that are located near these boundaries. The areas shown in **Figure 5-6** can be interpreted as areas with physical edges that are located in the general vicinity of boundaries among socially defined neighborhoods. The fact that these edges reside near officially identified neighborhood boundaries gives them social significance. The boundaries of neighborhoods delineated in Exercise 1 could also be used.

Step 3: Classify edges into two types.

It is important to analyze whether the edge areas identified above function as seams joining two neighborhoods, or as edges that filter or block something undesirable.

One approach for doing this is to determine who/what occupies the areas immediately adjacent to each edge. Then consider whether the surrounding functions are appropriate for the edge conditions encountered. For example, is there housing immediately adjacent to a barrier condition? Are there resilient uses adjacent to the edge, or are the uses more sensitive? **Figure 5-7** shows the northeast corner of Portage Park, where a highway defines its boundary. There, residences in yellow are located very close to a strong edge—a highway and rail line. This is an example of an edge surrounded by incompatible uses.

Based on this information, classify the edge areas according to two types: seams or filters. Edges that function more like seams than filters are those that draw two sides together. They may be less abrupt and "soft," and therefore able to encourage movement across. Edge areas that function—or should function—as filters are those located near something undesirable. The edge should act as a useful barrier or filter that softens the impact on surrounding residences and workplaces. There should be a form of protection, especially wherever nonresilient uses like housing are located near a noxious or other undesirable land use. The edge may function as a hard boundary and prohibit cross movement. As a form of protection, the edge may be necessarily impenetrable.

The shaded areas in **Figure 5-8** show the delineation of both types of edge areas (filters and seams).

FIGURE 5-8

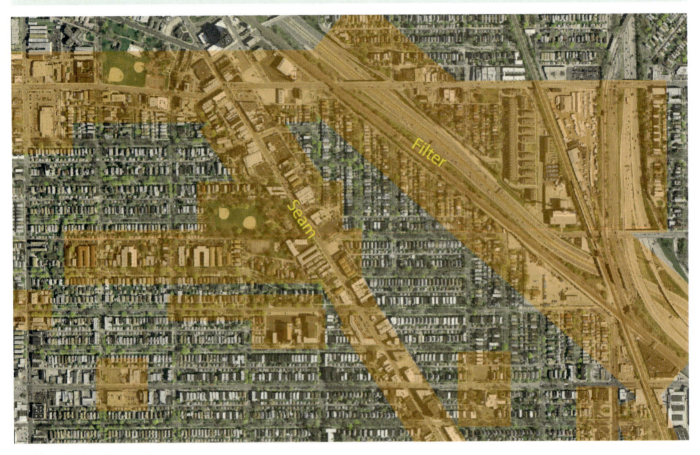

Two types of edges: filters and seams.

FIGURE 5-9

An edge area in Portage Park. Sketch by Elif Tural.

FIGURE 5-10

Selections for design intervention: three filters and three seams.

Edge as seam I: binding two sides of a strong edge.

Step 4: Visit each type of edge.

Observe enough of the edge so that it is possible to adequately characterize it to someone who has never been there. Observations should be recorded using sketches and photography. An example sketch of an edge area is shown in **Figure 5-9**.

Record observations by answering the following questions:
- Were the predictions based on the mapped, two-dimensional analysis correct? Does the area function as a filter or seam, or does the edge exhibit aspects of both types? Key questions in this regard are whether it was possible to cross the edge, or whether the edge was in fact a hard boundary and barrier. Does the edge function as a form of protection from something detrimental, or, if the area was classified as a seam, is there evidence of two sides coming together?
- What kind of emotions do these edge areas elicit? Do they feel threatening or unsafe, or is there a sense of calm? Is there a feeling of wanting to avoid them, move through them quickly, or move through them slowly?
- Does the space have any ambiance? Are there places to sit and rest? If so, would anyone want to sit there, or are the amenities essentially ornamental?
- Are there any activities or people in the area? Do the activities seem out of the ordinary, or routine?

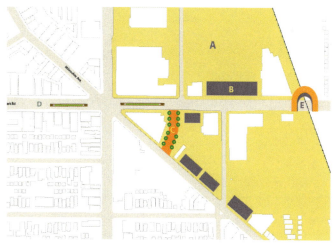

Edge as seam II: integrating an industrial corridor.

- Are there sidewalks going to the space and connecting it to surrounding areas? Should the edge have better connectivity around and through it?

Steps 1 through 4 can now be used to identify three types of filters and three types of seams. The six selected areas are shown in **Figure 5-10**. The selected sites, representing different types of edge areas, can now be used to propose specific, alternative design intervention strategies.

DESIGN

Step 5: Propose alternative interventions for edge areas.
Seams

The strategy for the first set of edges could be to increase their role as seams, promoting integration opportunities on multiple sides. There are opportunities to articulate openings and design them as functional and deliberate pathways that connect to the edge.

Figure 5-11 is an edge composed of a wide arterial that does not have any use as a "filter" but should instead be functioning like a seam, integrating the two surrounding areas. The area is located at the juncture between two neighborhoods, and thus has a special role to play in both delineating and drawing the areas together.

This can be accomplished by redefining the edge as an area that neighborhoods on both sides of the arterial are likely to use. A row of street trees could be added to compliment the disciplined

FIGURE 5-13

Edge as seam III: integrating a "trapped" residential area.

FIGURE 5-14

FIGURE 5-15

Edge as filter II: adding resilient uses.

Edge as filter I: inserting a greenway and connecting two small parks.

FIGURE 5-16

Edge as filter III: a bike path embraces the edge.

frontage of single-family homes on the east side. At point A, there is an entrance designed solely for cars, and this acts as a significant divider between the large campus buildings and the adjacent neighborhood. This entrance could be redesigned with a strong crosswalk to encourage cross movement. A small square could also be inserted there, transforming the entrance from its current function as a leftover space intended to buffer the entering cars to a usable civic space intended to serve both neighborhoods.

Figure 5-12 is an edge area made up of a hodgepodge of industrial corridors (the area in yellow), large vacant parcels, and parking lots, all adjacent to residential buildings. It also marks the boundary between two neighborhoods. Unfortunately, this edge is disruptive rather than integrative. It surrounds one of the busiest retail sections of the community (known as "six corners"), which is also the subject of an ongoing revitalization effort. It is thus an unfortunate location for a strong edge. Instead, the edge could be made to function more like a seam, drawing the surrounding areas together.

The industrial corridor at point A could be turned into an asset. Instead of treating it as discarded space that is ignored as one drives (quickly) through, blocks could be given special treatment (with sidewalk paving, artwork, or landscaping, for example) to give the area a unique identity as a light industrial corridor, perhaps one geared especially to family-run businesses. At point B, liner buildings could be encouraged to house light industry along both streets, as a way of giving spatial definition to the street and integrating the edge. A pedestrian pathway connecting the two main streets could be provided at point C, where the existing green patch in front of the building is transformed into a deliberate pedestrian connector.

Along Irving Park Road, the center turning lane could be replaced with a median. This softens the intersection, which is currently a wide arterial that is difficult for pedestrians to cross. Finally, to better integrate the whole area (including the six corners retail area, the industrial corridor, and the adjoining residential neighborhood), a gateway could be provided (with pillars or other markers on either side of the street, for example) that announces the area and lets passersby know that this section of Portage Park, edge and all, is part of the community.

Figure 5-13 is composed of a group of edges surrounding a residential section. The residences are "trapped" by edges on all sides, creating a good opportunity to introduce spaces that connect through and transform the edges to seams rather than barriers.

The design suggests tying the edges together by creating a seam that connects a new square at point C, along the railway, to the neighborhood at point A. The square could be designed to take advantage of its exposure to the railway, transforming it from an industrial dead-end to a unique type of civic space. Public art in this location would be especially appropriate. Articulate the spaces along the way by encouraging liner buildings at point B, and adding trees and planting strips at the other end, near the new square.

Filters

The strategy for this group of edges is to make them function more as filters, protecting the adjacent areas from their harmful effects.

Figure 5-14 shows a strong linear edge, a railroad, and a highway corridor, sitting right next to a residential area. This area could be better designed by lining the corridor—making the space useful as a recreational area, and acknowledging its role as an edge but also transforming it into a neighborhood asset.

A straightforward strategy would be to line the edge with a greenway. A "greenway" is a vegetated corridor of land that is used for recreation (walking, biking, jogging, and skating). It not only connects people and places but it can act as a protective filter. It could follow the railroad line and include benches and small garden spaces along the way. Ideally, the greenway would be connected to a larger regional system of greenways and parks. At a minimum, it could connect small new parks at points A and B, which are currently used as industrial storage sites.

Figure 5-15 is an example of an area where the surrounding edge is composed of large spaces that could be made to function more like filters than underutilized, dead spaces—a "no-man's-land" sitting right next to a dense residential neighborhood. One strategy would be to add resilient uses like offices, artist spaces, or light industry and small businesses as buffers wherever space allows. These would be uses that would not require a lot of drive-by traffic or parking, but would provide a needed buffer between the residential neighborhood and the highway/rail corridor.

The yellow area shown in **Figure 5-16** is an industrial corridor adjacent to residences. It is one of those areas that, in the shadow of a strong industrial edge, has turned into a hodgepodge of disconnected urban fabric, creating difficult, unusable spaces for local residents.

It would be possible to tie the area together, address the strong edge, and in the process present a more effective buffer for the residential areas by creating a small, linear park on one end (along the rail line) and then inserting a bike path that works its way through the neighborhood to connect to the park. This would help activate the edge, making it more usable. The connection would be enhanced by using a regularized planting scheme (that is, rows of trees that bind the spaces together and help define the bike path).

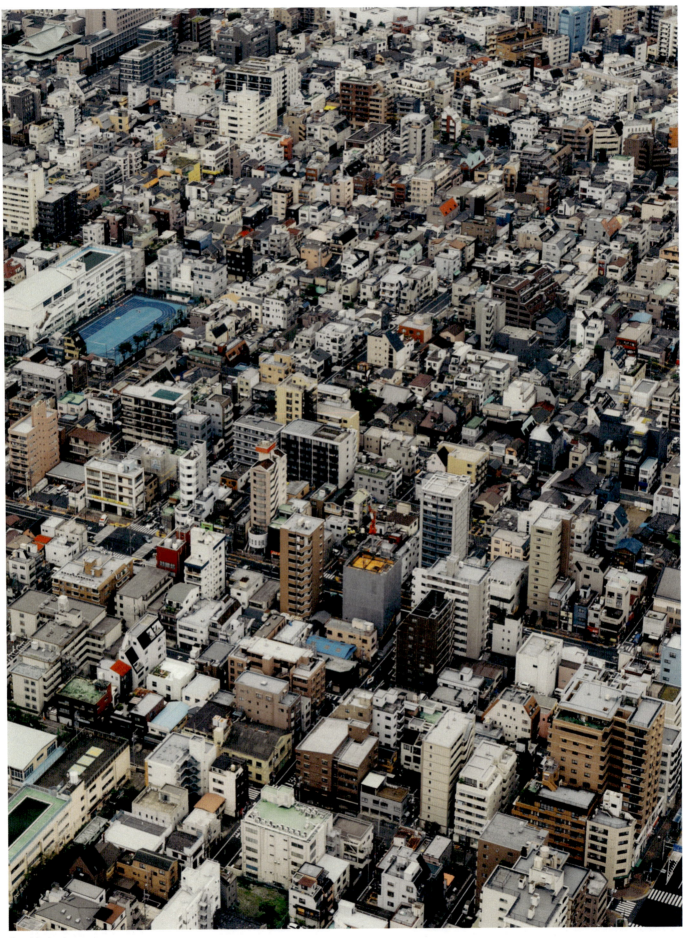

Sumida-ku, Japan.
Credit: Dawid Sobolewski

EXERCISE 6
MIX

Purpose: To evaluate land-use diversity in a neighborhood and propose design interventions that would support and enhance a healthy mix

BACKGROUND

Planners often argue that neighborhoods should be socially and economically diverse—mixed in income, mixed in use, and actively supportive of places that commingle people of different races, ethnicities, genders, ages, occupations, and households. New urbanists, smart growth advocates, creative class adherents, and sustainability theorists all have espoused the fundamental goal that a diversity of people and functions should be spatially mixed. In the realm of urban design, the basic idea is this: "the combinations of mixtures of activities, not separate uses, are the key to successful urban places" (Montgomery, 1998, p. 98). Quality in the built environment is routinely measured on the basis of variety, choice, and interest. The maximizing of "exchange possibilities," both economic and social, is viewed as the key factor of urban quality of life (Greenberg, 1995). More simply, the mixture of housing, schools, and shopping has been used as the basic definition of a good pedestrian neighborhood (Hayden, 2003).

Diversity of uses is seen as being crucial for good urbanism because it puts people and their daily life needs in proximity, thereby increasing the accessibility of urban places. Jane Jacobs argued most persuasively that land-use diversity is an essential ingredient of good urbanism. What counted for Jacobs was the "everyday, ordinary performance in mixing people," forming complex "pools of use" that would be capable of producing something greater than the sum of their parts (1961, pp. 164-5).

Lewis Mumford often wrote about the importance of social and economic mix, citing the "many-sided urban environment" as one with more possibilities for "the higher forms of human achievement" (1938, p. 486). Planners, in their plans for the physical design of cities, were supposed to foster this wherever possible to achieve the mature city: "A plan that does not further a daily intermixture of people, classes, activities, works against the best interests of maturity" (Mumford, 1968, p. 39).

Unfortunately, most observers would agree that, in the U.S., the mixing of uses—including housing types—has been in decline for a century, spawned in large part by the widespread adoption of land-use zoning regulations that began to proliferate starting in the 1920s. The separation of urbanism into components—abstracted calculations like land-use categories, miles of highways, square footage of office space, park acreage per capita—lead to, as Mumford termed it, the "anti-city" (1968, p. 128). Jacobs similarly berated planners for treating the city as a series of calculations and measurable abstractions that rendered it a problem of "disorganized complexity," and made planners falsely believe that they could effectively manipulate its individualized parts (1961).

The solution for urban designers is to foster a "close-grained" diversity of uses that provides "constant mutual support," whereby the focus is on, as Jacobs put, "the science and art of catalyzing and nourishing these close-grained working relationships" (Id., p. 14). The diversity must be substantive, not superficial. A commercial street that looks garish and chaotic is most likely not diverse but homogeneous. Venturi et al. (1977) discovered that architecture will attempt to present a sense of variety by being exhibitionist in the midst of an underlying homogeneity. Extreme variations in color, form, and texture are buildings crying out to be recognized amid an overbearing pattern of sameness.

ANALYSIS

Mix is measured by determining the spatial clustering of different types of land uses within a defined area. The designer can investigate the range of uses that exist in one locale (for example, within a pedestrian shed of a five- or 10-minute walking radius—a quarter to a half mile). If land uses are all the same in a given area, mix will be low, indicating that the area is homogeneous and lacking in diversity. Alternatively, a heterogeneous zone will be composed of a wide range of land uses within a confined area, indicating a high level of diversity.

Patterns of land uses, of course, are only one part of the analysis. A key question to be investigated is whether or not the urban form accommodates a mix of uses, especially a range of housing types.

Step 1: Find areas with different kinds and levels of mix.

There are many different ways to define mix. One strategy is to use different definitions and scales of mix, and overlay them to investigate whether certain areas stay mixed under different definitions. Data by parcel and data by census unit could both be used to determine mix.

Two layers—land use by parcel and housing type by block group—enable different interpretations of the spatial distributions of mix within a community. **Figure 6-1** shows land-use mix by parcel. The land-use categories used to make the map are shown in the key. Four areas, outlined in light blue, identify areas with a pattern of mix that is worth investigating for possible design intervention. These areas are not necessarily the ones with the most mix, which tend to be areas around the main commercial corridors. Instead, these are areas away from the main commercial corridors that nevertheless have an interesting mix of activities in a relatively small area.

Potentially, these could be important "seeds" for urban diversity for the community as a whole. For this reason, they are most likely areas that are worth preserving and enhancing via design intervention. Another reason to focus on these mixed use areas is that, because they are near strong retail activity, they may

FIGURE 6-1

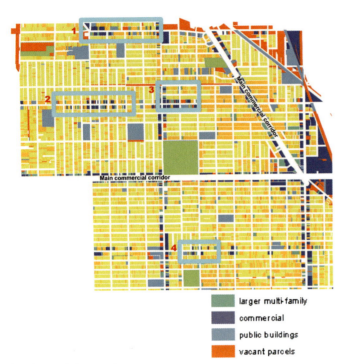

- larger multi-family
- commercial
- public buildings
- vacant parcels

Land-use mix by parcel.

FIGURE 6-2

Housing-type mix by census block group.

FIGURE 6-3

Housing-type mix by parcel.

FIGURE 6-4

Housing-type mix by parcel and census. (Figures 6-2 and 6-3 combined.)

be less vulnerable to loss of mix. Land-use mix in these locations is not likely to be contested by residents who want to keep things homogeneous.

Figure 6-2 identifies areas with the highest housing-type mix by census block group—areas 1 through 4. This is based on census data on unit type. Mix was determined by applying a diversity index. In this case, two different indices were used and combined to produce a composite measure of unit-type diversity.1

Step 2: Identify areas with low mix.

Figure 6-4 is composed of an overlay of two maps. The first, **Figure 6-3**, is a map of housing-unit type by parcel. It emphasizes the variation of housing type at the smallest spatial scale. The variation includes number of stories and number of units in one building. This map is overlaid with the map of census unit variation of housing type, **Figure 6-2**, to produce **Figure 6-4**. Thus, **Figure 6-4** is meant to show the location of areas with low housing mix measured in two different ways: by parcel and by census data. Three areas are identified as being particularly homogeneous when it comes to housing type.

DESIGN

How could urban design be used to help foster greater mix—or strengthen existing mix—in those areas identified above?

Step 3: Use design elements to strengthen areas with existing mix.

In areas of mix that are away from the main commercial corridors and may serve as important seeds of diversity (identified in Step 1 above), design elements can be inserted to provide a more supportive, strengthened environment. The main design ideas are motivated by the need to connect and infill transitional spaces. In addition, "leftover spaces" in alleys and vacant lots can be activated by inserting small, nonresidential uses like small retail, live/work units and other types of flexible, modular units.

Figures 6-5a, 6-5b, and **6-5c** correspond to areas 1, 2 and 3 on **Figure 6-1**. In each, modest interventions are proposed to help sustain and bind the mix shown on the inset maps. **Figure 6-5a** includes planting in the strip mall parking lot (point A), a small pocket-park insertion on a vacant lot (point B), upgraded crosswalks, and the insertion of street trees in locations where trees are currently missing.

Figure 6-5b shows a commercial area embedded in a residential section. There are certain weaknesses immediately apparent. The main intersection in this strategic area is weakly defined, basically consisting of vacant space on all four corners. This would be a good area to upgrade, installing planting strips (point B), crosswalks

The Policy Side

There are a number of policy and programmatic issues that go hand in hand with the design interventions suggested in this book. This is especially true in the case of housing-type mix.

The guiding principle in the interventions regarding mix is that the added units and uses should lead to greater, not less, social diversity. Most importantly, the interventions should not lead to displacement in the neighborhood; they should instead promote stability. Such goals will most likely require policy intervention.

Careful monitoring of change will be crucial. What are the effects of design interventions on specific populations? Are the needs of some groups—the young, the old, working parents, the poor, ethnic groups, households of different types—being accommodated or affected by the proposed interventions? Are there overlapping constituencies that will be simultaneously provided for, or is one group being attended to at the expense of another?

Areas with high mix in terms of building form but low social mix are probably areas that need policy intervention. Such intervention is likely to include strategies to retain housing affordability, or provide incentives for the development of new, affordable units. If these areas are already designed for mix in terms of form (such as providing a range of unit sizes and types), then the problem is not design, but policy. What may be needed are, for example, tax abatements, public subsidies for housing assistance, and nonprofit sector involvement (land trusts, self-help programs, micro-lending, and community development corporation activities).

(point C), and incentives for infill development (point A).

Figure 6-5c shows blocks with mixed uses on both sides of a residential area, but there are "holes" in the surrounding commercial fabric. The design interventions are focused on connecting the residential area to the commercial uses more effectively and more deliberately. There are access points between the residential areas and the commercial uses, but they are ad hoc—cutting through parking lots and navigating between buildings where pedestrian pathways seem an afterthought.

Intervention (point A) makes use of a vacant lot to construct a small plaza. This lot is already used to access the commercial uses; the intervention calls for legitimizing and strengthening this connection. Point B suggests some infill buildings to strengthen the

FIGURE 6-5A

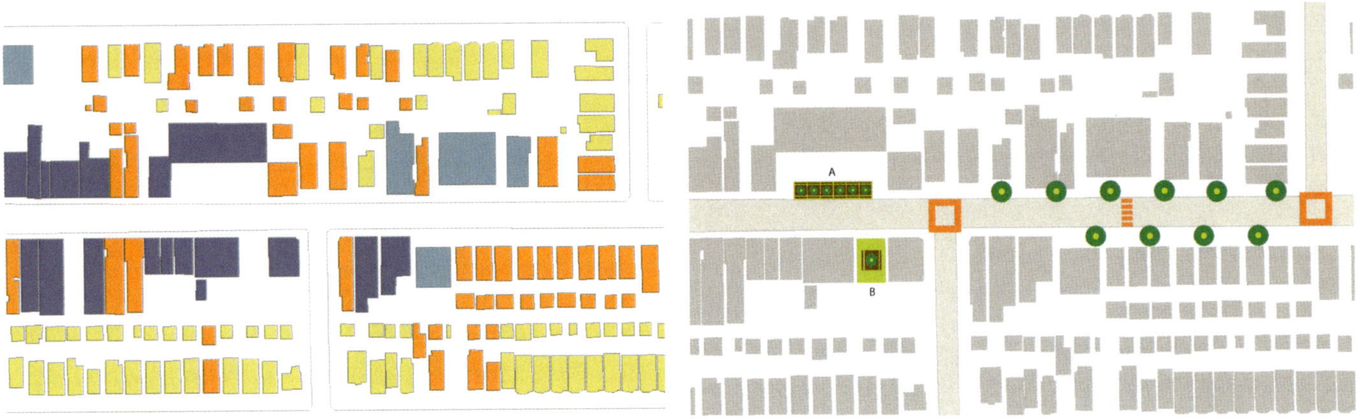

FIGURE 6-5B

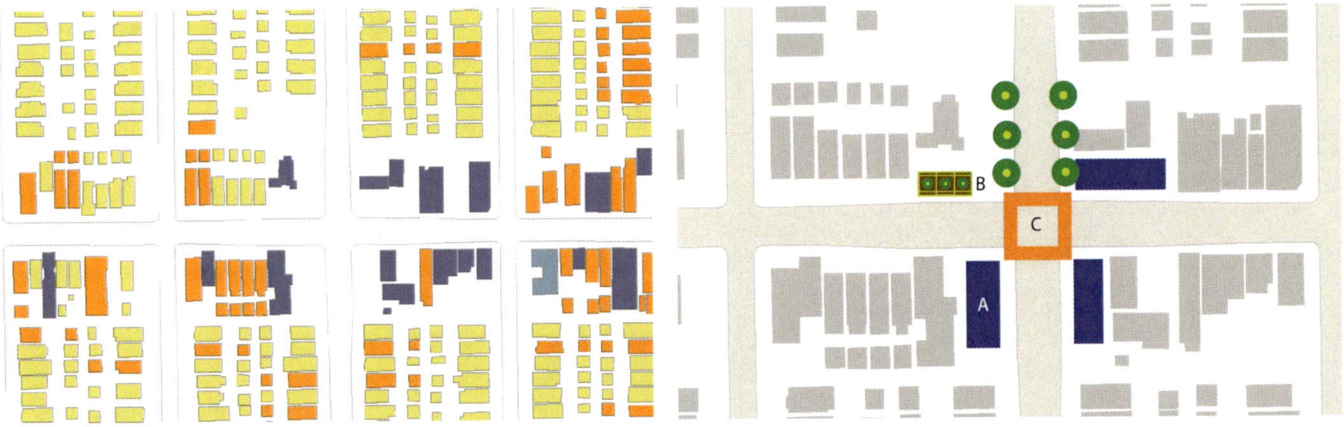

FIGURE 6-5C

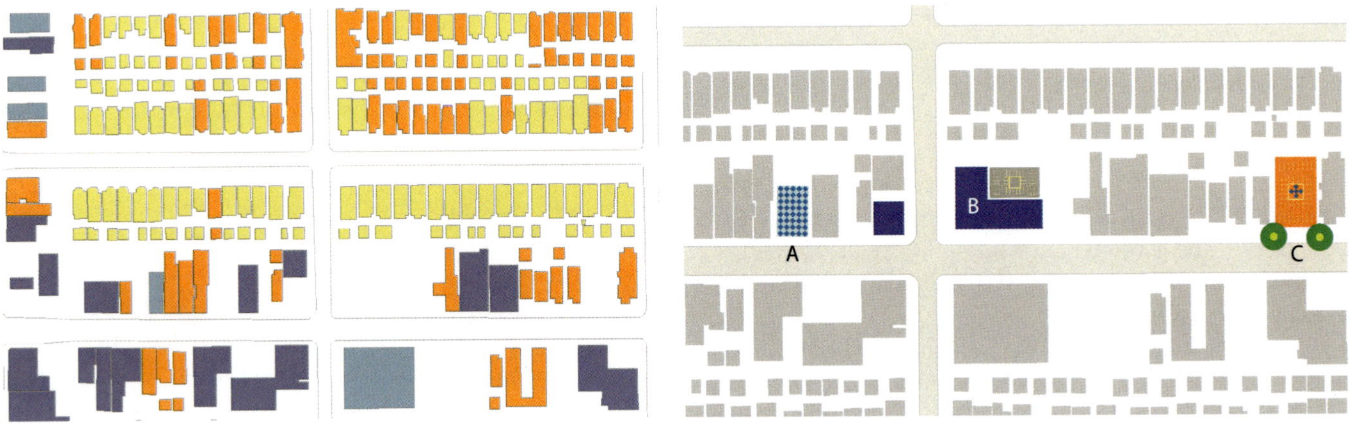

Modest interventions to sustain and bind the mix: three examples.

FIGURE 6-6

Upgrading the parking lots attached to nonresidential buildings in a residential area.

FIGURE 6-7

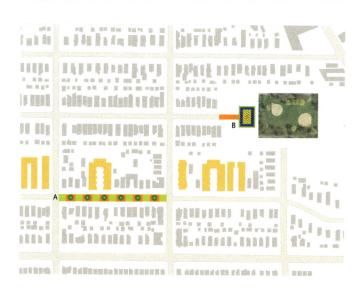

Strategies to support high housing-type mix.

FIGURE 6-8

A neighborhood pocket park system helps bind this high mix area together.

FIGURE 6-9

Anchor a key intersection in a high-mix area currently overrun with parking lots.

FIGURE 6-10

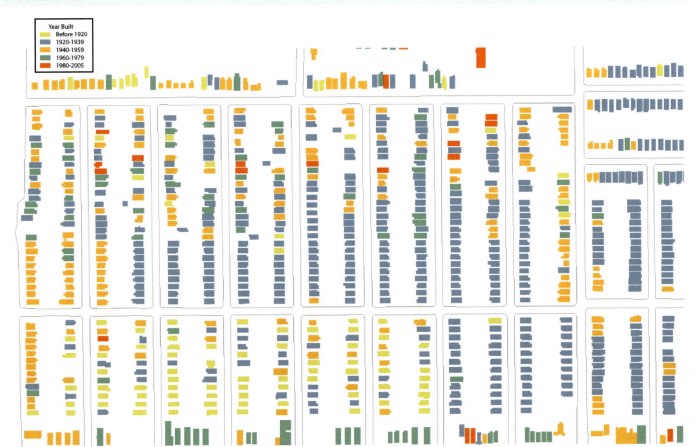

Underlying diversity in a seemingly homogeneous neighborhood I: building age.

commercial area at the corners, with parking behind. Finally, point C is an attempt to acknowledge the ad hoc path that has developed between the residential area and the street—currently through a parking lot—by formalizing the entrance with street trees.

Finally, in this group, the buildings shown in blue in **Figure 6-6** are nonresidential buildings, each of which has undefined open space attached (parking lots). The area should be valued as a place where nonresidential uses are well interspersed with residential. To strengthen the location, upgrade the open space attached to each nonresidential property by adding something desirable, like a row of trees.

Step 4: Strengthen areas with high housing-type mix.

Two interventions could be proposed for highly built-out areas with a high degree of housing-type mix: develop transitional spaces, and ensure that whatever public space exists is multipurpose and well connected to the surrounding area.

Start by looking for transitional spaces in areas with a high level of housing mix, identified in Step 1 above. In some areas, woonerfs ("streets for living," which accommodate both people and cars) can be developed among housing types. **Figure 6-7** is an example. Note the location of new condominiums in this area, highlighted in yellow. These new condos are surrounded by other types of housing, making this a good location to try to support the mix by providing an integrative public space (a woonerf at point A) that can accommodate multiple types of activities.

Also in this location is a public park dominated by two baseball diamonds. Given the high degree of housing-type mix, the residences should have very clear and direct linkages to this park, including a well-defined entrance (point B). Also consider making the park more multipurpose and multigenerational, adding both sitting areas and playground equipment in addition to sports fields.

Figure 6-8 shows an area of high housing mix with very little existing public space. There are small spaces that could be linked, perhaps with some common feature or neighborhood marking system—an element to connect these small spaces and give the sense that there is a public realm weaving its way through this diverse neighborhood. Shown is a series of small pocket parks, which could have a common design theme that links them together.

Figure 4-14 from the centers exercise (Exercise 4) was an area of high mix with very little public space. Transforming the parking lot there into a multipurpose space for a marketplace, farmers market, or other civic function would be beneficial not only to the idea of creating a center but also to the goal of supporting the mix surrounding it.

Finally, **Figure 6-9** is an area of parking lots surrounded by a high level of housing mix. Since not all of these parking lots can hope to be redeveloped at the same time in order to revitalize the commercial corridor, it would be useful to at least create a focal point at the main intersection, providing sidewalk treatment and anchoring the four corners with buildings. The intersection could be targeted as one where traffic-calming measures would be particularly important, in order to provide a better pedestrian environment and a way of stabilizing the surrounding mix.

Step 5: Propose design strategies for areas of low housing mix.

In areas of low housing mix, identified in Step 2 above, two strategies are important. First, look for alternative ways of defining and locating mix, then acknowledge and build on it. One strategy would be to make sure existing codes aren't undermining these alternative types of mix. For example, **Figures 6-10** and **6-11** show the underlying mix of area 1 identified on **Figure 6-4**. They both show that, despite being identified as homogeneous, area 1 actually has some underlying diversity, if diversity is defined in a particular way. Defining diversity based on building age (**Figure 6-10**) or on the basis of number of stories in addition to unit type (**Figure 6-11**) reveals a certain complexity that could be strengthened by ensuring that codes do not hold this kind of diversity in nonconformance.

Second, show the possibilities for infill housing that are simultaneously compatible with both single-family and multifamily housing. **Figure 6-12** shows that—even in homogeneous, built-up neighborhoods—there are always some lots open, as shown in orange on each map. These should be targeted as locations to propose new housing development that is compatible with multiple housing types. Four possibilities are shown. These are example units that would fit in well with single-family environments, and could be used to lessen fears about incompatible housing type and density. Another infill possibility in a predominantly single-family residential area is the bungalow court, shown in **Figure 6-13**.

FIGURE 6-11

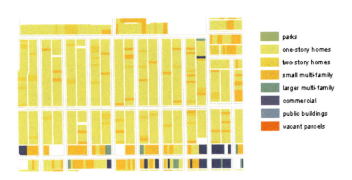

Underlying diversity in a seemingly homogeneous neighborhood II: number of stories.

FIGURE 6-13

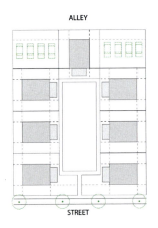

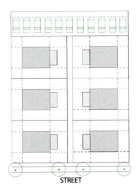

A bungalow court is compatible with single-family housing. Drawing inspired by an affordable housing project designed by John Anderson of New Urban Builders (Chico, CA).

FIGURE 6-12

Open lots in a single-family neighborhood: infill strategies. SketchUp models courtesy of Opticos Design, Inc.

Malacca, Malaysia.
Credit: Peter Nguyen

EXERCISE 7
PROXIMITY

Purpose: *To evaluate distances between where people live and what people need, and to propose design interventions that would help increase desirable proximities*

BACKGROUND

One aspect of the urban environment on which there seems to be some agreement—at least from the ranks of smart growth advocates, sustainable development proponents, and new urbanists—is that urban areas ought to strive for better proximities between where people live and work and the goods and services they require for a high quality of life.

Proximity is essentially about access. "Access" can be formally defined as the quality of having interaction with, or passage to, a particular good, service, or facility. This has been a longstanding component of theories about good urban form (see in particular Lynch, 1981, and Jacobs and Appleyard, 1987). Most notably, Kevin Lynch (1981) held access as a key component of his theory of ideal urban form. In the broadest sense, Lynch argued that access could be used as a measure of "settlement performance" (a measure of what makes a "good" city) by factoring in the feature to which access is being given and the person receiving access.[1]

Proximity (or access) to facilities, goods, and services is what differentiates urban sprawl from compact city form: development patterns that are low density and scattered necessarily diminish accessibility because facilities tend to be far apart and land uses are segregated (Ewing, 1997). There is also the issue of equity: who has access to a particular good or service and who does not, and whether there is any pattern to these varying levels of access.

Proximity in urban planning and design is about evaluating the ability to reach urban places, and the quantity and quality of places that can be reached. The first part could be a simple count of the number of facilities within a given area such as a census tract, or it could be the distance (cost) between an origin and one or more destinations. In addition to understanding who has access to what, urban designers will want to consider the socioeconomic characteristics of a population. An important consideration is that, for locally oriented populations (such as elderly and poor residents who rely on modes of transport other than the automobile), accessibility to urban services may be significantly more important (Wekerle, 1985).

Since residents with fewer resources are likely to benefit most from greater proximity to daily life needs, design that promotes better proximities for dependent or disadvantaged populations should be a key concern to urban designers. In particular, lower-income residents are more dependent on public transit, have lower access to private automobiles, and therefore require greater access. For residents in such locations, lower levels of proximity are particularly detrimental.

ANALYSIS

Proximity can be assessed by measuring the distance of one set of locations to another. For urban design purposes, the best approach is to select a set of urban facilities or places to which access is important, and then evaluate distances throughout the neighborhood to those facilities or places. In addition, some decisions should be made about who should have access to what facilities, as a matter of addressing equity.

Step 1: Find areas that have low versus high access to the most desirable facilities and places.

Identify the facilities that would be most desirable to be near, and then find areas that have low versus high access to these places. Some of these were already identified during the neighborhoods and centers exercises (Exercises 1 and 4, respectively). Obvious choices are public schools, libraries, and parks.

Draw a buffer around each place (either by hand, or by using a GIS buffering tool). Use a distance of a quarter mile, which is generally assumed to be the distance people can readily walk within five minutes. **Figure 7-1** is a map showing the selected locations in Portage Park (public schools, parks, and libraries) and a quarter-mile radius around each. Areas within the yellow buffer have good access; areas in white do not.

FIGURE 7-1

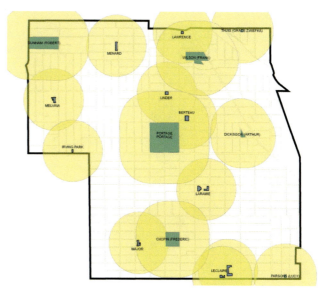

Areas with good access to parks, schools, and libraries.

FIGURE 7-2

social diversity   % under 18   % over 65   density   median income

Spatial patterns of sociodemographic variables in Portage Park. Darker areas have higher levels for all variables except income. For median income, darker areas have lower income.

FIGURE 7-3

Areas with good access to parks, schools, and libraries.

FIGURE 7-4

Red spaces are vacant lots in the commercial area where there is high need and low proximity.

NOTE

From these basic categories, Lynch delineated a large number of additional complexities (for example, the flow of information, access variation by time and season, the fact that access is not always a quantity to be maximized, the need to be able to shut off the flow of access, perception of access, and the benefits of moving to as well as arriving at a given destination).

Step 2: Identify high-priority areas.

"High-priority areas" are areas that would most benefit by being proximal to the desirable facilities and places identified above. Overlay the following layers to identify target locations:

- Areas of high population density
- Areas of high social diversity
- Areas of low income
- Areas with a lot of children
- Areas with a lot of seniors

These are the places that should have the best proximity to the most desirable facilities/places. To find areas that satisfy one or more of these conditions, census data can be used. The series of maps shown in black and white in **Figure 7-2** indicate the distribution for each variable by census block group. For each variable or map, darkly shaded areas are high priority—that is, darker shades have higher density, higher social diversity, lower income, higher children, and higher numbers of seniors. The trick is to find those areas with the most need on the most number of variables.

There are many different ways to interpret these maps. Each census area could receive a score (for example, 1 through 5, depending on the shade of gray), and then the scores for each variable could be added together to get a composite score for each block group. A slightly more sophisticated approach would be to give each layer a weighted score (for example, if the community determined that low income was a more important variable to consider than density).

Another approach, used here, is to find those block groups that are in the highest category of need for at least two criteria. All block groups in red on **Figure 7-3** are areas that had high need (shaded darkest) on two or more variables. The map combines this information with the proximity layer, showing those areas that simultaneously have high need but low proximity (red areas that are not covered by yellow shading). These are the areas on which urban designers could focus in order to increase access.

Step 3: Identify sites where amenities, services, and facilities should be added.

Within those areas that do not have good access to the most desirable facilities and places, and yet have high need, find locations that could be potential sites for targeted public investment.

Figure 7-4 is a map showing a major commercial strip running through the underserved area in Portage Park (identified in **Figure 7-3**). The vacant lots within this commercial area could be targeted as locations where public assets would have the greatest impact.

DESIGN

Step 4: Propose infill strategies.

Design intervention that tries to increase proximity involves finding the most important sites for development and proposing new infill for those locations. Such infill could include any number of new neighborhood-serving uses.

Figures 7-5 and **7-6** show two strategies for infill. The first map identifies all the areas that could be developed as commercial space. The most important strategy here would be to provide incentives for neighborhood-serving retail in those locations. The second map shows some suggestions for inserting public spaces—plazas that double as parking lots (when warranted), small formal parks, public squares, and planting strips. These are just a few of the possible uses that could be very valuable in this area of high-need, low-proximity, and high-vacant land. Any combination of neighborhood-serving retail and public space could be targeted in a nonresidential corridor like this.

FIGURE 7-5

Incentivize commercial infill in areas with high need and low proximity.

FIGURE 7-6

Strategically placed public amenities in areas of high need and low proximity.

Curitiba, Brazil.
Credit: Rodrigo Kugnharski

GROUP 3
RECURRENT ISSUES

Recurrent design issues and how to handle them.

There are certain issues in urban design that are especially recurrent. Three of the most common—density, parking, and traffic—are generally regarded as problems to be solved rather than assets to be strengthened or preserved. Often, however, these issues can be turned into assets rather than problems by applying good design principles:

- **DENSITY**: Density, if designed right, should be regarded as a community asset.

- **PARKING**: The storage of cars can be detrimental to neighborhoods, but design can mitigate the negative effects.

- **TRAFFIC**: High-traffic areas should be calmed in urban neighborhoods; the needs of pedestrians should be paramount.

Redondo Beach, California. Credit: Paul

EXERCISE 8
DENSITY

Purpose: *To show how neighborhoods can increase in density in ways that are not harmful but beneficial*

BACKGROUND

Density has become a hot topic in the U.S. More people seem to realize that the American dream of a single-family house on its own lot is not sustainable in the long term. There is a sense that our low-density settlement patterns are going to have to change; that we need to learn how to live more compactly and reduce our dependence on cars. That means finding ways to accept and welcome density. Julie Campoli and Alex MacLean make the case in their book Visualizing Density (2007), arguing that we can learn to love density by understanding that its negative effects—crowding and monotony—are the result of bad design, not density per se.

For development in existing neighborhoods (infill), the problem is that higher-density developments are seen as a threat to single-family homes and property values. This is why design is so critical—good design for infill housing that increases density embeds the infill within a larger context. Such designs take on the expanded goal of ensuring that it is possible to "envision each building, each development project, in relation to a positive ideal" (Brain, 2005, p. 32).

Design for increased density is critical for residents to be able to visualize the trade-offs involved. They need to see how density is not always about detracting, but actually helps create better public spaces, retain essential services they might deem important, sustain a walkable environment, and, potentially, keep housing more affordable.

Where density may be thought of as being too high, the problem may be one of crowding rather than density. Jane Jacobs (1961) made the distinction between crowding and concentration, arguing that crowding was an unhealthy condition that had to do with too many people per room. Concentration, on the other hand, was necessary for good urbanism. Jacobs was advocating something in the range of 100 dwelling units per acre, which is very dense by American standards, but the distinction between crowding and concentration is still applicable in many contexts.

The mix exercise (Exercise 6) already showed strategies for mixing housing types in single-family neighborhoods. It showed possibilities for infill housing that is compatible with both single-family and multifamily housing simultaneously. Four possibilities were shown of units that would fit in well with single-family neighborhoods, but there are other ways in which density can be increased in existing neighborhoods.

In addition to apartment buildings and high rises that respect existing neighborhood contexts, there is the possibility of allowing corner duplexes, walk-up apartments on side streets, accessory units over garages, and housing above stores. The first step is to provide a rationale for increasing density in some locations.

Often, the increase in density is a matter of incorporating and integrating small units like accessory units or "granny flats." Small-unit integration is especially important because it provides options for low- to moderate-income households, as well as additional rental income for existing property owners. Housing can be fit into the open spaces of single-family lots. Housing over commercial space is another important strategy. It's not only smaller and therefore likely to be more affordable but it has the added value of providing more client base for small business owners in the vicinity.

Increasing density can also be a matter of innovative types of multifamily housing; courtyards and closes (short, looped streets with housing around them) are examples. Early 20th century

FIGURE 8-1

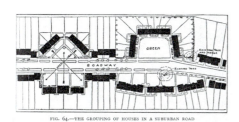

H. Inigo Triggs, 1909. *Town Planning: Past, Present and Possible*, p. 195.

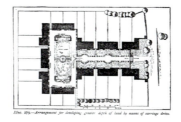

Raymond Unwin, 1909. *Town Planning in Practice*, p. 353.

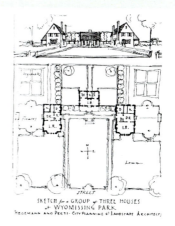

Werner Hegemann & Elbert Peets, 1922. *The American Vitruvius: An Architects' Handbook of Civic Art*, p. 213.

Housing infill strategies, early 20th century.

FIGURE 8-2

Parcels close to civic spaces.

FIGURE 8-3

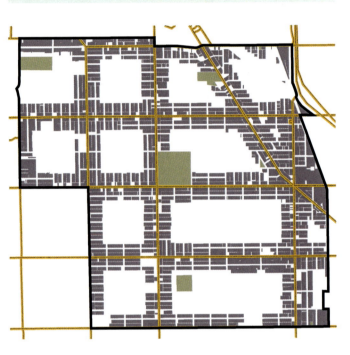

Parcels close to transit (bus, rail) and commercial uses.

FIGURE 8-4

Available space: open land near civic, transit, and commercial uses.

FIGURE 8-5

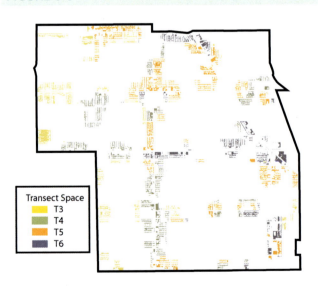

Transect Space
- T3
- T4
- T5
- T6

Available space by transect zone.

FIGURE 8-6

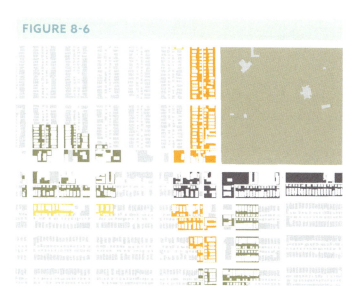

Around Portage Park: available space by transect zone.

Garden City designers like Raymond Unwin were especially good at fitting in attached row houses among single-family housing. Three examples from planning textbooks are shown in **Figure 8-1**.

ANALYSIS

Start the analysis with two basic assumptions. First, density should be higher in certain places and lower in others. Second, the way in which an increase in density can be accommodated varies with the location. Some locations can increase density with a simple accessory building in the rear, while other locations can accommodate a full apartment block. Not every block can gracefully accommodate a higher-density building; different types of units are appropriate in different contexts.

Where would an increase in density be most suitable? Three kinds of locations stand out. Density should be higher around civic institutions, commercial areas, and public transit. The first two locations were selected because such locations provide the public amenities and services that higher-density living requires. A town house requires a town (that is, good access to facilities of various kinds). In a sense, higher-density living, accompanied by lower amounts of private space, should be "rewarded" with greater access to public space and facilities. Of course, the reward needs to be worthwhile. There should be access to worthwhile things like neighborhood-level services, stores and facilities, and valued civic institutions.

The idea that higher densities should be encouraged in places near public transit is based on several factors. The first idea has to do with parking. Sometimes residents object to allowing increased density because of a (real or perceived) increase in cars in the area. Tying the provision of more units to areas well served by transit can lessen this impact, as well as lessen the cost burden of car ownership. New units should be encouraged in areas close to transit—possibly even with parking restrictions, not requirements. Another reason for increasing density near transit lines is that an increase in density supports public transport, resulting in higher ridership and, potentially, greater efficiencies.

After delineating areas that are both close to civic institutions and commercial areas and near public transit, the second step is to determine how the suggested increases in density vary with locational context. For that determination, it is necessary to go back to the transect zones mapped out in Exercise 2.

Step 1: Find areas that are close to civic uses, commercial areas, and public transit.

Identify locations that provide an amenity like a civic institution (schools and parks), are near commercial retail space, and are close to transit. **Figure 8-2** shows all parcels that are clustered around civic spaces. **Figure 8-3** shows parcels close to transit (bus) lines and commercial retail land uses. In both maps, a very short distance was used—500 feet, or about a two- to three-minute walk. **Figure 8-4** combines these two layers to locate all parcels that satisfy all conditions—close to civic, commercial, and transit. This figure also whites out the buildings on each parcel. The resulting map shows open land in these locations—potentially, land that can accommodate more density. Note, however, that density increases obviously are not restricted to open land (and could instead involve adding on to existing structures).

Step 2: Determine the transect zone for each area.

To determine the kind of density appropriate for a given location, overlay the available spaces from Step 1 with each transect zone identified in the transects exercise (Exercise 2). **Figure 8-5** shows the available space for each transect zone, and **Figure 8-6** gives a detail of the area around Portage Park (the large park in the center of the Portage Park community). In the detail, there are four different intensity levels (transect zones) and each level will correspond to a different kind of infill development.

Step 3: Determine what kinds of units would be appropriate in each location.

Each transect zone supports a different kind of density. To get a sense of this variation, examine the residential types in the SmartCode that correspond to each zone. Use these to suggest infill development strategies appropriate to a particular block. As an example, **Figure 8-7** shows four types of units and the transect zones in which they could be located.

DESIGN

In the design phase, specific locations where each building type could reasonably be added are proposed. The goal is to demonstrate density under a range of conditions, using locations and corresponding building types identified in Step 3.

Figure 8-8 shows different infill options. The figure shows how different types of units, corresponding to different densities, could fit into different transect zones in targeted areas.

FIGURE 8-7

Accessory unit
T3, T4, T5

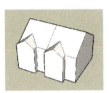
Live/work units
T3, T4, T5, T6

Courtyard housing
T3, T4

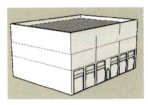
Mixed use block
T5, T6

Housing infill strategies and corresponding transect zones. SketchUp models courtesy of Opticos Design, Inc.

FIGURE 8-8

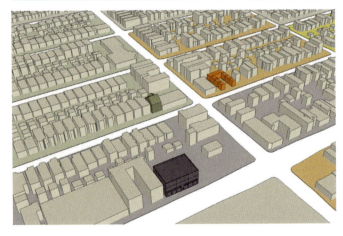

Increasing density based on transect intensity levels.

Atlantic City, New Jersey.
Credit: Tim Trad

EXERCISE 9
PARKING

Purpose: *To propose design strategies that minimize the negative effects of parking*

BACKGROUND

In 1944, Jose Luis Sert lamented in his planning manifesto, Can Our Cities Survive?, that the "absence of parking space" meant that "the city motorist can no longer drive up to the place where he wishes to go." Such sentiments have changed, at least among urban designers and planners. Most everyone agrees that abundant parking space has been highly destructive to urban neighborhoods, leading to poor design quality and disruption of pedestrian access. Now, the goal of planners is to put parking behind, under, or above buildings; on the street; or in parking structures rather than lots. The importance of dealing with the storage of cars has led some urbanists to proclaim that "urbanism starts with the location of the parking lot" (www.citycomforts.com).

Many people have studied and written about the destructiveness of parking. Donald Shoup argued in his book, The High Cost of Free Parking (2005), that free parking has led to a host of ills—from high energy use and environmental degradation to a damaged economy and financial strain. It is a self-propelling destruction, as more parking requires more driving, which in turn requires more parking. This, Jane Jacobs argued, was also a function of diversity: "Lack of wide ranges of concentrated diversity can put people into automobiles for almost all their needs. The spaces required for roads and for parking spread everything out still farther, and lead to still greater uses of vehicles" (p. 230).

Planners from the early 20th century—roughly as soon as cars started to become a problem—had some good ideas about how to handle the storage of cars. Often, the solution for car storage took place in the context of a planned "automobile suburb." A highly regarded example is Mariemont (outside of Cincinnati, Ohio), planned by John Nolen and developed by Mary Emery in 1918. It was one of the first suburban developments to consciously accommodate the automobile by providing parking areas and garages in a way that did not detract from the overall quality of the place.

Another example is the way in which parking was integrated into apartments and office buildings, often in ways that did not detract from the frontage quality of the street (see **figure 9-1**). Developments like these offer valuable models of automobile accommodation that keep disruptive tendencies of car storage in check.

Parking lots that front streets also have a way of lessening security. When people walk along sidewalks fronted by parking lots, they feel vulnerable—a problem Jane Jacobs wrote about extensively. This in turn compromises the economic health of commercial corridors, which, to stay viable, need residents and visitors to feel secure in them. To strengthen security of commercial corridors, streets should be lined with active uses rather than "dead space" like parking lots.

Broadly speaking, the responses to mitigating the negative effects of parking areas fall into four categories:

FIGURE 9-1

Creative car storage. Source: Daniel Zack.

1. Eliminating the parking lot and developing the lot as something else, thus losing the parking space (and possibly replacing the lost spaces elsewhere, such as on the street);
2. Making parking lots more habitable and even utilizing them as public open space while still retaining parking;
3. Buffering the lot with landscape or buildings; and
4. Developing them as mixed use parking structures with retail or office space as frontage.

Examples are shown below.

The first option is to simply remove parking lots that front streets. The parking might be eliminated altogether, or it could be replaced with on-street parking or parking in some other location. Of course, this would require changing the minimum parking requirements in the zoning code, something that has been accomplished in places like Portland, Oregon. There, rules specify maximum instead of minimum parking spaces. In addition, parking requirements can be location-specific. The authors of Suburban Nation (Duany, Plater-Zyberk, and Speck, 2000) argue for the differentiation of "A" and "B" streets, where the first is

FIGURE 9-2

Humanizing a parking lot with active uses. Source: Sucher (2003).

FIGURE 9-4

A capital-intensive solution: parking above and retail below. Source: Louis Meuler.

FIGURE 9-3

Parking buffered by planting.

FIGURE 9-5

Within 500 feet of a neighborhood center, much land is given over to the storage of cars (area in red).

primary and restricts fronting by parking lots, while the second is less restrictive about frontage.

Second, there is the notion that planners can "reclaim and people" parking lots. In the book, City Comforts: How to Build an Urban Village, David Sucher (2003) shows an example of a supermarket with a parking lot in front (see **Figure 9-2**), transformed into a public space—first selling plants, then coffee, then adding chairs and tables.

Another example in this category is the case of a plaza that functions simultaneously as a parking lot. As shown in **Figure 4-10**, these dual-purpose spaces are found throughout Europe, where plazas from many time periods have been made to function as parking areas, with little loss in the quality of space. Often, such spaces are blessed with a location where buildings front the space on all sides, creating an outdoor room. With the addition of better paving materials, and an identifying feature like a fountain, a parking lot can be transformed to function as a public space while still providing parking. The parking lot can even function as a neighborhood center if it is connected to other public spaces and redesigned to function as an integrated space.

The third way to respond to the problem of parking lots is to buffer them with something more pedestrian-friendly. This varies from simple landscaping to something much more substantial. The main idea is to hide the parking area by putting it behind or to the side of a building. **Figure 9-3** shows the simple solution of covering up a parking area with a planting strip. This is a minimal solution, but preferable to no buffering at all.

Finally, parking lots can be viewed as developable property, to be replaced with a more active use like retail, or even office space, and with a garage incorporated. This solution is much more substantial, and will be capital-intensive. However, it is also highly desirable because it retains the existing parking while adding a more active, pedestrian-oriented use. **Figure 9-4** shows the incorporation of retail below a parking structure. Here, the parking has been placed above, lessening its effect on the public realm while at the same time adding more parking capacity.

While many planners and residents can appreciate the high costs of parking, few in the U.S. are advocating the "car-free" city, as has sometimes been attempted (successfully) in Europe. It is of course necessary to address the interrelationship that exists between land use and transportation, because this ultimately affects the need for more parking. There will always be a need for some cars in cities, and the design issue remains: How can cars be stored in a way that minimizes their destruction of the public realm? Fortunately, a wide number of interesting ideas have been proposed. Some of these strategies, most of which take parking as a given rather than as a phenomenon that can be eliminated, will be applied in this exercise.

ANALYSIS

Step 1: Find parking lots located in strategic places.

The first step is to find parking lots that, because of their location, can do the most damage. One strategy would be to start with the neighborhood centers identified in the centers exercise (Exercise 4). As the most strategic places in the neighborhood, what areas within them have excessive space given over to cars and the storage of cars? Exercise 4 identified spaces where a significant and diverse population crossed paths. These are exactly the spaces—key intersections at major streets—where parking lots are likely to have the most negative effect.

Figure 9-5 shows the amount of area given over to the storage of cars in some of the neighborhood centers in the northern section of Portage Park (including alleys, but excluding streets and on-street parking). Only the parking areas within 500 feet of the intersection are highlighted. Even within this tight spatial limit, the amount of red space is significant—and detrimental. In most cases, it covers more than half of the land around the center.

Step 2: Select one of four parking lot options for each area.

In the areas around these centers, identify and categorize where the four parking lot options identified above might be most applicable. Differentiate four possibilities: eliminate, convert, buffer, or develop. **Figure 9-6** shows the layers used and the four locations selected in the analysis. Criteria and examples are shown below.

Option 1: Eliminate the existing lot. Replace the parking with a building or public space, and put the existing parking somewhere else, off-site. Replacement with on-street parking may be the most preferable replacement option.

This option may be best where an existing lot is underutilized and there doesn't seem to be a great need for a parking lot in that location (the parking lot may be there by default rather than market demand or definite need). This can be determined by counting the number of spaces regularly used in the lot at different times of the day.

Area 1 on **Figure 9-6** is a good example. This intersection includes Portage Park on one corner and a car dealership across from it, but there is another corner taken up by a parking lot that is not fully used. Given the proximity to an important public space, in addition to the underutilization of the lot, this parking lot would be a good candidate for elimination.

Option 2: Convert the parking lot to a usable small retail or public space, while still retaining the parking function. This could range from incorporating small, informal retail spaces in a parking lot (as shown in **Figure 9-2**) to conversion to a plaza that doubles as a parking area during peak times (see **Figure 4-10**).

FIGURE 9-6

Four options for solving the parking lot problem. High population density blocks and existing public space are also shown.

FIGURE 9-7

The parking structure option may be appropriate where there is a high usage lot with public space nearby.

For the strategy involving conversion to small-scale retail, this option may work best in small spaces, such as in between buildings. These are spaces that aren't large enough, or don't have enough traffic, to justify the building of an entirely new development, like a mixed use retail building with a garage attached (Option 4). Nevertheless, the parking lot frontage is damaging because people have to walk through it or past it to get to shopping.

Conversion to a plaza may work best wherever there is a need for public space in the area. Ideally, the location would also be near high-density residential areas so that as many residents as possible would be able to take advantage of the public space created. Two additional layers, then, are needed to analyze the possibility of converting a parking lot to a plaza:

1. Existing public open space (to look for locations deficient in public open space); and
2. Population density (to look for high-density areas)

The plaza conversion option may also work well in front of a strip mall, which may have a parking lot that is too shallow to incorporate a new building. Repaving, so that the lot could function as a multipurpose parking lot/civic space, may be the preferred option.

Area 2 on **Figure 9-6** is a good example of the kind of parking lot that needs to keep its parking function but, at the same time, could benefit from a more concerted effort to humanize the space. As shown on the map, this is an area of relative high density (dark gray blocks), but with few civic spaces in the immediate vicinity (green areas). Parking is needed but, given the density and lack of civic space, there is a rationale for considering the conversion option.

Option 3: Buffer the parking lot. In some cases, the goal may be to hide the parking lot completely, while, in other cases, a more realistic goal would be to simply reduce the negative visual impact. This depends on whether the parking lot is necessary for a retail establishment, or if it is simply a lot being used by employees, in which case the lot could be shielded completely and there would be no need to advertise its location. Buffering options commonly include simple landscaping, such as a planting strip or row of trees. Around the entrance to a parking lot, buffering could also include bulbouts, whereby the entry is narrowed and pedestrian crossing is improved.

The buffering option is likely to occur wherever parking structures cannot be developed, or where there is strong resistance to the capital investment required for other design options. Investment in the more intensive options will be less feasible in areas that are only weakly developed or where the population density is low. In such places, the most that can be hoped for is probably a mitigation of the negative visual impact of the parking lot by adding a landscape buffer.

Area 3 on **Figure 9-6** is a good candidate for this option. The blocks shaded light gray have a low residential density, thus making the construction of a parking garage, new building, or even repaving (as in Option 2) hard to justify. A more modest option would be to simply add a planting strip or other landscape buffer.

Option 4: Develop the parking lot. This option is reserved for heavily used lots. Start with parking lots located in T5 or T6 zones to identify areas with the most intensity. Additionally, new garage/retail development would be most appropriate in areas that need more parking in order to sustain surrounding uses. This may be relevant for public as well as retail uses. For example, development could be appropriate for lots that front a well-used public space currently lacking in sufficient nearby retail opportunities, or in an area that could absorb additional retail uses. Parks and schools are good examples of well-used public spaces that may be in need of adjacent retail (as well as parking capacity). In either case—near a public space or near existing retail—the strategy would be to take advantage of the existing foot traffic that is currently underserved by retail, while at the same time providing needed parking.

While new structures to replace parking lots are generally reserved for locations that lack adequate parking, there is an important caveat: Almost everyone in almost every city is likely to claim the need for more parking—it's the most common request planners get! Therefore, there is a need to be selective and discriminating—only the most trafficked places are capable of generating enough usage to justify a parking structure.

Area 4 on **Figure 9-6** shows the location of a parking lot that meets these criteria. This is a high-intensity area (retail and residential) with a high-usage parking lot. It is near T5 and T6 zones and, as the detail in **Figure 9-7** shows, there is a public space—a baseball field—just down the block that could also justify the need for a parking structure.

DESIGN

Step 3: Compare the design options for a strategically located parking lot.

Determining which parking option to choose is not always straightforward. Taking one strategic site in Portage Park (the lot adjacent to the park at the center of the community, labeled "1" on **Figure 9-6**), three interventions can be visualized in order to compare the design options. The parking lot is underutilized, despite being across the street from one of the main public assets in this community.

Figure 9-8 shows the lot eliminated and parking replaced with on-street parking near the existing site. The lot could be developed

FIGURE 9-8

Option 2: convert the lot using small retail.

as a retail space or office building with parking behind, accessed at the side. On-street parking is also added—just a few spaces at the front of the building to indicate that parking in the area does exist. Sometimes just the suggestion of available parking adjacent to a retailer—not necessarily one-for-one replacement—is enough to entice someone to circle around and park nearby rather than next to the building.

It is important to note that the street may need to be reconfigured to accommodate this option. **Figure 9-9** shows an example of how the street could be reconfigured to accommodate more parking. Here, two lanes with a center turning lane have been slightly reworked in order to accommodate on-street parking lanes on both sides.1

Figure 9-10 is an example where the existing parking lot is retained, but the lot is given some pedestrian focal points in order to lessen the negative impact of parked cars. The design intervention is modest, providing only some outdoor seating areas and small retail stands. Although the parking lot is retained, the addition of outdoor seating and retail activates and humanizes the space. Adding landscaping (trees and other greenery) would help soften the parking lot.

Figure 9-11 shows a set of design interventions for the area labeled "2" on **Figure 9-6**. The idea in this case is to combine two parking lot redesign strategies, both of which rely on retaining

FIGURE 9-9

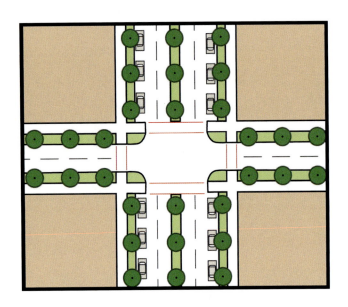

Option 1 requires reconfiguring the street to accommodate more parking.

FIGURE 9-10

Option 2: convert the lot using small retail.

FIGURE 9-11

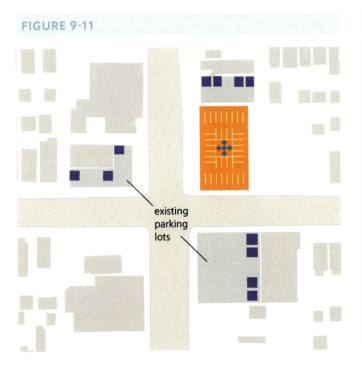

Option 2: convert a cluster of lots using small retail (kiosks and newsstands), adjacent to a parking plaza.

FIGURE 9-12

Option 3: buffer the lot.

parking but converting the space into something more pedestrian-oriented. In this example, a civic space is created by converting the large parking lot at the corner into a plaza. Upgraded paving materials and a central feature like a fountain help to transform the space. Nearby, small retail spaces (newsstands, kiosks) are added in front of strip malls and other retail establishments fronted by large parking lots. The success of these small spaces, still embedded in existing parking lots, is likely to be helped by their proximity to the parking plaza. A network of unconventional parking lots is therefore created at this intersection, without loss of existing parking capacity. An added incentive is that this area is weak in terms of existing public space.

Figure 9-12 is an example where the existing parking lot has been retained, but this time the lot is softened with a row of street trees. This is a minimalist intervention, but one that could be realistically accomplished. Residents, with the help of urban designers, only need to know how to make the case.

Finally, there is the option of parking lot development such as the example shown in **Figure 9-4**. If there is an area of high use and high density near a civic space—as shown in **Figure 9-7**—then the insertion of a parking structure may be a justified design option. The structure should include retail on the ground floor and parking above or below. If parking structures are lined with active uses, they contribute rather than detract from the public realm.

For this kind of capital-intensive project, it is first necessary to determine the number of spaces that could be accommodated in the new structure, since the extra capacity will relieve parking lot requirements from surrounding areas at least within a five-minute walk. A four-story structure can accommodate approximately 250 cars, which would not only accommodate all existing surface parking shown but would absorb parking pressure in the surrounding areas.

NOTE

The dimensions for these designs are based on two sources: the SmartCode and Context Sensitive Solutions in Designing Major Urban Thoroughfares for Walkable Communities (Institute of Transportation Engineers, 2005).

Shanghai, China.
Credit: Denys Nevozhai

EXERCISE 10
TRAFFIC

Purpose: To find locations where excessive traffic is diminishing neighborhood quality, and to propose design strategies that would help mitigate traffic problems

BACKGROUND

Cities have always struggled to accommodate the needs of pedestrians and the needs of wheeled vehicles simultaneously. The problem became acute when the number of cars on city streets rose exponentially in the early 20th century. At first, the relationship between cars and cities was romanticized. Tony Garnier laid out his futuristic Cité Industrielle in Paris in 1904, proposing a "machine-age community" of hydroelectric plants, aerodomes, and highways, all strictly segregated according to function (LeGates and Stout, 1998, p. xxxi). The proposal launched generations of planners and architects who envisioned a world of functional clarity, while underestimating the effect such separation was likely to have on the quality of place.

Separation of land uses has an obvious effect on traffic generation: the more separated things are, the less walking is possible and the more driving is required. Modernist ideas about urbanism that reached full flowering by the 1950s—ideas that had the effect of increasing traffic on urban streets—included not only the separation of land uses but the accommodation of the automobile in the form of high-speed highways, and the rejection of the street as an important part of the public realm and, with it, the rejection of street life.

The focus on designing for cars, speed, and unimpeded flow has constituted a narrow conceptualization of settlement that has discounted the complexity of cities and human behavior. Especially tragic has been the view that city streets could be widened and turned into fast-moving arterials to accommodate suburbanites fleeing the city—at the expense of inner city neighborhoods.

Proclamations from the 1940s that "the insufficient width of streets causes congestion" and that "distances between cross-streets are too short" (Sert, 1994, pp. 170, 174) have by now been largely discredited because such proclamations fail to account for the effect of wide streets on neighborhood quality and the needs of pedestrians.

By the late 20th century, the focus had shifted toward a concern for pedestrian life, walking, and the ways in which urban traffic can be made less disruptive. This has in part been motivated by a concern over the effect of the built environment on physical activity and human health. Streets that are pedestrian-oriented are believed to have an effect not only on quality of place but on the degree to which people are willing to walk. Researchers have argued that activity levels can be increased by implementing small-scale interventions in local neighborhood environments (Sallis, Bauman, and Pratt, 1998).

A whole catalog of design strategies are used to make streets—especially ones that are overly trafficked—more pedestrian-oriented. Many of these strategies fall under the heading "traffic calming." The concept is relatively recent, probably originating with the Dutch "woonerf" in the 1970s. Since then, traffic calming has been promoted as a way to reduce vehicle speeds, reduce accidents involving cars and pedestrians, and lower noise levels and air pollution. The effect of traffic calming on pedestrian quality and improving the public realm is a more specific orientation and motivation of urban designers.

According to the Institute for Transport Studies at the University of Leeds, England (www.highlands.com/pdra/reports/eurorept.html), traffic-calming measures on main roads in urban areas generally consist of:

- Narrowing, including pedestrian crossing points
- Islands and medians
- Tree planting

Aspects of these traffic-calming measures may be incorporated in the creation of multiway boulevards, avenues, and boulevard streets (see "Boulevard" in glossary).

ANALYSIS

Urban designers can play a crucial role in mitigating the effects of excessive traffic. As with many of the other exercises, the analysis involves first determining where attention should be focused—in this case, streets where traffic calming is likely to be most needed.

Focus on three conditions:

1. Streets with potential conflict between local and through traffic;
2. Wide streets where the pedestrian realm is less that 50 percent of the total right-of-way; and
3. Wide streets with heavy traffic that also contain a high volume of pedestrians.

The first two conditions signal the possibility of creating a boulevard. The last condition warrants a variety of traffic-calming interventions.

Step 1: Identify streets attempting to carry both local and through traffic.

The attempt to accommodate both local and through traffic on the same street results in a potential conflict. Streets in this category are likely to be located where the following conditions overlap:

- Streets that are near, or that traverse;
- Predominantly residential areas with predominantly local traffic; and

Traffic-Calming Measures

There are a number of websites and resources available that give examples of "traffic-calming" measures. Usually, these are within the context of promoting "pedestrian-friendly streets," "active living," or "walkable communities."

Particularly well-known examples include:

- Project for Public Spaces (www.pps.org)
- America Walks (www.americawalks.org)
- Active Living by Design (www.activelivingbydesign.org)
- Dan Burden's Walkable Communities, Inc (www.walkable.org)

Dan Burden's Walkable Communities, Inc., is particularly useful because it provides a large selection of images that illustrate traffic-calming concepts (available at www.pedbikeimages.org). He provides examples of the following types of traffic-calming measures:

- Bike Lanes & Paths
- Bulbouts/Curb Extensions/Neckdowns
- Chicanes
- Choker
- Crosswalks
- Curb Radius & Intersection Reductions
- Curb Ramps
- Diverters
- Full- & Partial-Street Closures
- Gateways
- Lane Reduction
- Median & Refuge Island Paving Treatments
- Medians & Refuge Islands
- One-Way Street
- Pedestrian Malls
- Pervious Paving Treatments
- Raised Crossings
- Raised Intersections
- Roundabouts
- Sidewalks & Walkways
- Speed Cushions
- Speed Humps
- Speed Tables
- Street Trees
- Traditional Narrow Streets
- Unvegetated/Unplanted Medians
- Vegetated/Planted Medians
- Woonerf

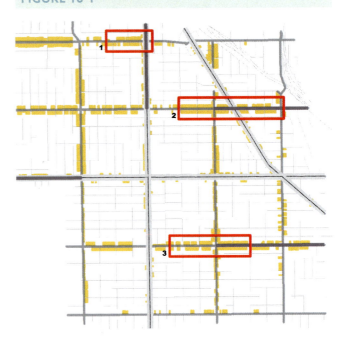

Potential conflicts: streets that carry local and through traffic. Yellow areas are residential parcels.

Wide streets with insufficient pedestrian realms.

- Streets that are also wide, with relatively heavy traffic, or that provide a regional connection.

These overlapping local and nonlocal conditions are likely to cause problems for pedestrians, and design intervention may be especially needed.

The following three layers of information can be used to locate these streets:

1. Wide streets with relatively heavy traffic;
2. Streets with regional connections (as shown in **Figure 3-2**); and
3. Residential parcels that front these streets.

Figure 10-1 shows three areas where the above three conditions are found. These areas are mostly fronted by residential parcels, and yet the streets are heavily trafficked due to their regional connections (essentially the main passages to places outside the neighborhood). In addition, the streets are fairly wide, generally greater than 80 feet in right-of-way width.

Step 2: Identify wide streets where the pedestrian realm is less than 50 percent of the total right-of-way.

According to The Boulevard Book: History, Evolution, Design of Multiway Boulevards (Jacobs, Macdonald, and Rofe, 2003), the pedestrian realm of a boulevard should make up at least 50 percent of the total right-of-way. Streets identified in this step have the potential width to become avenues or boulevards, but the pedestrian realm is relatively weak. Conversion to an avenue or boulevard is especially warranted given the subpar percentage devoted to pedestrian use.

Figure 10-2 shows two areas that have the potential to be designed as avenues or boulevards. The right-of-way ranges from 65 to 100 feet wide, but their pedestrian realm is subpar. In addition, they are not immediately fronted by single-family residential uses, but are fronted by a mix of land uses.

Step 3: Identify streets that simultaneously have a high volume of pedestrians and are significantly wide and traffic-congested.

The following layers can be used to make this determination:

- Wide streets with relatively heavy traffic
- Areas that have high residential density and that have high numbers of people who are likely to rely more on walking:
    - Areas of low-income and high-rental units
    - Areas with a lot of children
- Areas with a lot of seniors

Figure 10-3 shows three areas that meet all of the above conditions. The darker shaded areas (census block groups) have relatively lower income and higher rental, plus have relatively higher levels of children (under 18) and seniors (over 65).

Step 4: Identify transect zone locations.

Finally, overlay the above information with the map of transect zones (**Figure 2-8**) to determine the appropriate street context for traffic-calming measures. The design phase will use traffic-calming features—road narrowing, islands and medians, and tree planting—to create or improve one of four thoroughfare types (a street, a commercial street, an avenue, or a boulevard) identified in the SmartCode.

Figure 10-4 shows transect zones and street right-of-ways, and identifies four locations for design interventions. These represent four different traffic-calming contexts. As with the parking exercise (Exercise 9), the dimensions for these designs are based on two sources: the SmartCode and Context Sensitive Solutions in Designing Major Urban Thoroughfares for Walkable Communities (Institute of Transportation Engineers, 2005).

DESIGN

Design intervention to mitigate traffic problems involves first locating areas most in need of street redesign and traffic calming (Steps 1 to 4 above), and then determining the kind of thoroughfare redesign that would be most appropriate for that location. Thoroughfare type gives the appropriate dimensions for traffic-calming strategies.

The strategies presented here will focus on designing new thoroughfares appropriate to each location. Four examples are given: a street, a commercial street, an avenue, and a boulevard. The definitions can be summarized as follows (based on definitions found in the SmartCode; see glossary):

- Street: Low-speed, low-capacity urban thoroughfare with parking on one or both sides, raised curbs, and regularly spaced street trees.
- Commercial street: Low-speed urban thoroughfare with mostly commercial uses, moderate to high vehicular capacity, wide sidewalks, parking on both sides, and regularly spaced tree wells.
- Avenue: Low- to moderate-speed, high-capacity thoroughfare, often with a landscaped median; may function as a connecting thoroughfare among urban centers.

FIGURE 10-3

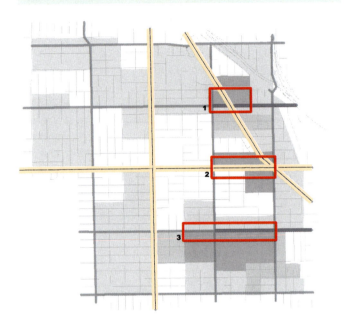

Potential conflicts: streets that carry local and through traffic. Yellow areas are residential parcels.

FIGURE 10-4

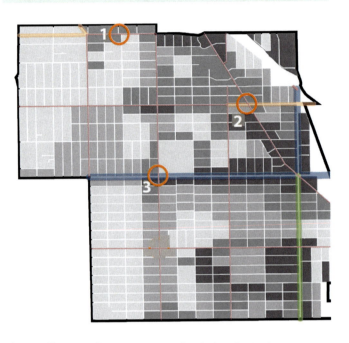

Three traffic issues. Transect zones and variations in street right-of-ways are shown.

FIGURE 10-5

Traffic calming in area 1.

FIGURE 10-6

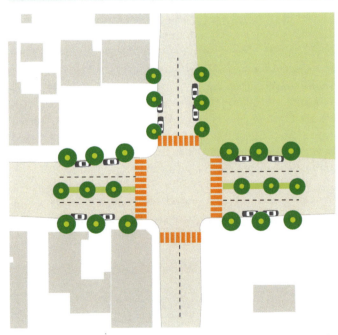

Thoroughfare redesign: a boulevard street.

- Boulevard: Moderate-speed, high-capacity thoroughfare, often with separate side roads for local traffic that buffer sidewalks and buildings. Sometimes there is a distinction between a "multiway boulevard," which separates local and regional traffic, and the "boulvard street," which is a landscaped thoroughfare without side streets (see Jacobs, Macdonald, and Rofe, 2003).

The SmartCode provides 22 typical thoroughfare assemblies, specifying, for example, appropriate public frontage, private frontage, and right-of-way and traffic lane width. Using these assemblies as a guide, the problem areas identified above can be redesigned to conform to one of these thoroughfare types. In addition, thoroughfares can be traffic-calmed using one or more of the following measures:

- Road narrowing, including pedestrian crossing points
- Parallel parking
- Islands and medians
- Tree planting, either continuous planters or tree wells
- Widened sidewalks

Step 5: Redesign thoroughfares in area 1.

Area 1 was identified in Step 1 as a mostly residential area with wide streets and a lot of traffic—definitely an area that needs to be calmed. Given the existing right-of-way and the transect zones through which it passes (T3, T4, and T5), a street assembly that is slow-moving (20 mph), with two lanes of traffic and a parking lane on either side, would be appropriate. An example of how this street would be detailed at an intersection is shown in **Figure 10-5**.

Area 4 is also mostly fronted by residential parcels, with wide streets and heavy traffic (Step 1), and has a high number of pedestrians (Step 3). Given its wider right-of-way, intervention would suggest more of an avenue assembly where, in addition to parking on both sides and a six-foot sidewalk, a seven-foot continuous planter could be added in the middle.

Step 6: Redesign thoroughfare in area 2.

Thoroughfare redesign for area 2 would entail slightly different configurations. The area was identified in Step 2 as having avenue or boulevard potential. There are two different configurations that would work well in the two locations shown. Although not wide enough to be a multiway boulevard, area 2 (a detail of which is shown in **Figure 10-6**) could accommodate the features of a "boulevard street," including two lanes of traffic, parking on both sides, and a continuous planter in the center. A three-dimensional view of the street redesigned as an avenue is shown in **Figure 10-7**.

Where there is a narrower right-of-way, the thoroughfare could be designed as a commercial street rather than a boulevard, with 13- to 15-foot sidewalks, parking on both sides, and regularly spaced tree wells.

FIGURE 10-7

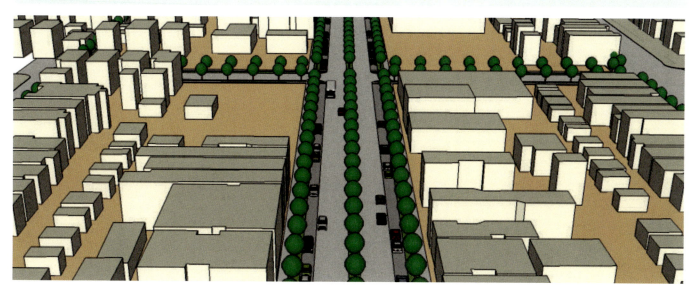

An axonometric view of the boulevard street shown in Figure 10-6.

URBAN DESIGN FOR PLANNERS

TOOLS, TECHNIQUES, AND STRATEGIES

EMILY TALEN

REFERENCES

Alexander, Christopher. 1965. "A City Is Not a Tree." *Architectural Forum* 122 (April): 58–62; and (May): 58–61.

Banerjee, Tridib, and William Baer. 1984. *Beyond the Neighborhood Unit: Residential Environments and Public Policy.* New York: Plenum Press.

Bingler, Steven, Linda Quinn, and Kevin Sullivan. 2003. *Schools as Centers of Community: A Citizens' Guide for Planning and Design.* Washington, D.C.: U.S. Department of Education. Available at www.edfacilities.org.

Brain, David. 2005. "From Good Neighborhoods to Sustainable Cities: Social Science and the Social Agenda of the New Urbanism." *International Regional Science Review* 28: 217–38.

Bussagli, Marco. 2004. "Buildings and Typologies." Pp. 40–75 in *Understanding Architecture, vol. 1.* Armonk, N.Y.: M. E. Sharpe.

Campoli, Julie, and Alex MacLean. 2007. *Visualizing Density.* Cambridge, Mass.: Lincoln Institute of Land Policy.

City of Longmont, Colorado. 2003. *Preservation of Undeveloped Land for Pocket Parks in Neighborhoods.* Available at www.ci.longmont.co.us/city_council/retreat/2003/pdfs/openspace.pdf.

Davidson, Michael, and Fay Dolnick, eds. 2004. *A Planners Dictionary.* PAS Report No. 521/522. Chicago: American Planning Association.

Dramstad, Wenche E., James D. Olson, and Richard T.T. Forman. 1997. *Landscape Ecology Principles in Landscape Architecture and Land-Use Planning.* Cambridge, Mass., and Washington, D.C.: Harvard University and Island Press.

Duany, Andres, Elizabeth Plater-Zyberk, and Jeff Speck. 2000. *Suburban Nation: The Rise of Sprawl and the Decline of the American Dream.* New York: North Point Press.

Duany, Andres, Elizabeth Plater-Zyberk, and Robert Alminana. 2003. *New Civic Art: Elements of Town Planning.* New York: Rizzoli.

Duany, Andres, Sandy Sorlien, and William Wright. 2008. T*he SmartCode version 9 and Manual.* Available at www.smartcodecentral.com.

Duany, Plater-Zyberk and Co. 1998. *The Lexicon of the New Urbanism.* Miami: Duany, Plater-Zyberk and Co.

Ewing, Reid. 1997. "Is Los Angeles-Style Sprawl Desirable?" *Journal of the American Planning Association* 63 (1): 107–26.

Farr, Douglas. 2007. *Sustainable Urbanism: Urban Design with Nature.* New York: Wiley.

Fischer, Claude S. 1982. *To Dwell Among Friends: Personal Networks in City and Town.* Chicago: University of Chicago Press.

Franck, Karen A., and Lynda H. Schneekloth, eds. 1994. *Ordering Space: Types in Architecture and Design.* New York: Van Nostrand Reinhold.

Gehl, Jan. 1987. *Life Between Buildings: Using Public Space.* New York: Van Nostrand Reinhold.

Gilroy, Rose, and Chris Booth. 1999. "Building an Infrastructure of Everyday Lives." *European Planning Studies* 7 (3): 307–25.

Grannis, Rick. 2003. "T-Communities: Pedestrian Street Networks and Residential Segregation in Chicago, Los Angeles, and New York." Working paper.

Greenberg, Mike. 1995. *The Poetics of Cities: Designing Neighborhoods That Work.* Columbus: Ohio State University Press.

Hayden, Dolores. 2003. *Building Suburbia: Green Fields and Urban Growth, 1820–2000.* New York: Pantheon Books.

Hegemann, Werner, and Elbert Peets. 1996 [1922]. *The American Vitruvius: An Architects' Handbook of Civic Art.* New York: Princeton Architectural Press.

Hillier, B., and J. Hanson. 1984. *The Social Logic of Space.* Cambridge: Cambridge University Press.

Hudnut, William H., III. 2003. *Halfway to Everywhere: A Portrait of America's First-Tier Suburbs.* Washington, D.C.: Urban Land Institute.

Institute of Transportation Engineers. 2005. *Context Sensitive Solutions in Designing Major Urban Thoroughfares for Walkable Communities.* Washington, D.C.:ITE.

Jacobs, Allan, and Donald Appleyard. 1987. "Toward an Urban Design Manifesto." *Journal of the American Planning Association* 53 (1): 112–20.

Jacobs, Allan B., Elizabeth Macdonald, and Yodan Rofe. 2003. *The Boulevard Book: History, Evolution, Design of Multiway Boulevards.* Cambridge, Mass.: MIT Press.

Jacobs, Jane. 1961. *The Death and Life of Great American Cities.* New York: Random House.

Kelbaugh, Doug. 1996. "Typology—An Architecture of Limits." *Architectural Theory Review* 1 (2): 33-52.

Krieger, Alex. 1999. "The Planner as Urban Designer: Reforming Planning Education for the Next Millennium." Pp. 207-9 in *The Profession of City Planning: Changes, Successes, Failures and Challenges (1950-2000),* ed. Lloyd Rodwin and Bishwapriva Sanyal. New Brunswick, N.J.: Center for Urban Policy Research.

LeGates, Richard, and Frederic Stout, eds. 1998. "Editor's Introduction." P. xxxi in *Early Urban Planning*, 1870-1940. New York: Routledge.

Los Angeles County Regional Planning District. 1941. *Master Plan of Highways of the County of Los Angeles, California.*

Lynch, Kevin. 1981. *Good City Form.* Cambridge, Mass.: MIT Press.

McHarg, Ian. 1969. *Design with Nature.* New York: Wiley.

Michaelson, W. 1977. *Environmental Choice, Human Behavior and Residential Satisfaction.* Oxford: Oxford University Press.

Montgomery, John. 1998. "Making a City: Urbanity, Vitality and Urban Design." *Journal of Urban Design* 3 (1): 93-116.

Mumford, Lewis. 1938. *The Culture of Cities.* London: Secker and Warburg.

———. 1968. *The Urban Prospect.* New York: Harcourt Brace Jovanovich.

Orfield, Myron, and Robert Puentes. 2002. *Valuing America's First Suburbs: A Policy Agenda for Older Suburbs in the Midwest.* Washington, D.C.: Brookings Institution.

Perry, Clarence Arthur. 1929. "The Neighborhood Unit." In *Neighborhood and Community Planning.* New York: Regional Plan of New York and Its Environs.

Rybczynski, Witold. 1999. "Where Have All the Planners Gone?" Pp. 210-16 in *The Profession of City Planning: Changes, Successes, Failures and Challenges* (1950-2000), ed. Lloyd Rodwin and Bishwapriva Sanyal. New Brunswick, N.J.: Center for Urban Policy Research.

St. Louis Great Streets Initiative. Available at www.greatstreetsstlouis.net/component/option,com_glossary.

Salingaros, Nikos A. 1998. "Theory of the Urban Web." *Journal of Urban Design* 3: 53-71.

Sallis, James F., Adrian Bauman, and Michael Pratt. 1998. "Environmental and Policy Interventions to Promote Physical Activity." *American Journal of Preventive Medicine* 15: 379-97.

Samuels, I., and L. Pattacini. 1997. "From Description to Prescription: Reflections on the use of a Morphological Approach in Design Guidance." *Urban Design International* 2 (2): 81-91.

Sert, Jose Luis. 1944. *Can Our Cities Survive? An ABC of Urban Problems, Their Analysis, Their Solutions.* Cambridge, Mass.: Harvard University Press.

Shoup, Donald. 2005. *The High Cost of Free Parking.* Chicago: APA Planners Press.

Skjaeveland, Oddvar, and Tommy Garling. 1997. "Effects of Interactional Space on Neighbouring." *Journal of Environmental Psychology* 17: 181-98.

Smith, Tara, Maurice Nelischer, and Nathan Perkins. 1997. "Quality of an Urban Community: A Framework for Understanding the Relationship Between Quality and Physical Form." *Landscape and Urban Planning* 39: 229-41.

Southworth, Michael, and Eran Ben-Joseph. 2003. *Streets and the Shaping of Towns and Cities.* Washington, D.C.: Island Press.

Sucher, David. 2003. *City Comforts: How to Build an Urban Village,* rev. ed. Available at www.citycomforts.com.

Talen, Emily. 2008. *Design for Diversity: Exploring Socially Mixed Neighborhoods.* London: Elsevier.

Unwin, Raymond. 1909. *Town Planning in Practice: An Introduction to the Art of Designing Cities and Suburbs.* London: T. Fisher Unwin.

U.S. Dept. of Transportation. "Glossary." *In Designing Sidewalks and Trails for Access.* Available at www. fhwa.dot.gov/environment/sidewalks/appb.htm.

Vanderburgh, David. 2003. "Typology." Pp. 1355–56 in E*ncyclopedia of 20th-Century Architecture,* vol. 3, ed. R. Stephen Sennott. New York: Routledge.

Venturi, Robert, Steven Izenour, and Denise Scott Brown. 1977. *Learning from Las Vegas: The Forgotten Symbolism of Architectural Form.* Cambridge, Mass.: MIT Press.

Walljasper, Jay, and the Project for Public Spaces. 2007. T*he Great Neighborhood Book, A Do-It-Yourself Guide to Placemaking.* New York: New Society Publishers.

Wekerle, Gerda R. 1985. "From Refuge to Service Center: Neighborhoods That Support Women." *Sociological Focus* 18 (2): 79–95.

Zelinka, Al, and Susan Jackson. 2006. *Placemaking on a Budget: Improving Small Towns, Neighborhoods, and Downtowns Without Spending a Lot of Money.* PAS Report No. 536. Chicago: American Planning Association.

GLOSSARY

This glossary is a very selective list of urban design terms, drawn from this book. There are four main sources for the definitions and images:

1. SC: SmartCode definition (Duany, Sorlien, and Wright, 2008)
2. PD: A Planners Dictionary (American Planning Association, 2004)
3. PPS: Project for Public Spaces (www.pps.org)
4. PBIC: Pedestrian and Bicycle Information Center (www.pedbikeimages.org)

Accessory unit: An apartment sharing owner-ship and utility connections with a principal building (SC).

Arcade: A private frontage conventional for retail use wherein the facade is a colonnade supporting habitable space that overlaps the sidewalk, while the façade at sidewalk level remains at the frontage line (SC). Image: PPS-Mizner Park, Boca Raton, FL. Image ID 40642.

Atrium: A ground-level area designed for pedestrians that meets the following conditions: (1) has at least one entrance connecting to a public street, plaza, or arcade; (2) is open to the top of the building by means of a vertical open space or light well, and is covered by a transparent or translucent material; (3) is open to the public during business hours; (4) has at least 25 percent of its periphery utilized by retail sales, personal services, or entertainment activities; and (5) contains facilities for the public, such as benches, flower beds, and fountains (PD). Image: PPS-ID 10884.

Avenue: A thoroughfare of high vehicular capacity and low to moderate speed, acting as a short distance connector between urban centers, and usually equipped with a landscaped median (SC).

Block: The aggregate of private lots, passages, rear alleys, and rear lanes, circumscribed by thoroughfares (SC).

Bollard: Vertical posts used to further reduce the "optical width" of a narrowed street, thereby discouraging speeding (PPS). Image: PPS-ID 29718.

Boulevard: A thoroughfare designed for high vehicular capacity and moderate speed, traversing an urbanized area. Boulevards are usually equipped with slip roads buffering sidewalks and buildings. If there are no slip (side) roads, they may be termed "boulevard street" (SC). Image: PBIC.

Bulbout: See curb extension. Image: PBIC.

Chicane: Sidewalk extensions that jog from one side of a street to the other to replicate such a circuitous route (PPS). Image: PBIC.

Choker: Extensions in selected areas (such as at intersections or at midblock) as opposed to a full sidewalk widening (PPS). Image: PBIC.

Civic building: A building operated by not-for-profit organizations dedicated to arts, culture, education, recreation, government, transit, and municipal parking, or for use approved by the legislative body (SC).

Civic space: An outdoor area dedicated for public use. Civic space types are defined by the combination of certain physical constants including the relationships among their intended use, their size, their landscaping, and their enfronting buildings (SC).

Civic: The term defining not-for-profit organizations dedicated to arts, culture, educa-tion, recreation, government, transit, and municipal parking (SC).

Commercial: The term collectively defining workplace, office, retail, and lodging functions (SC).

Configuration: The form of a building, based on its massing, private frontage, and height (SC).

Corridor: A lineal geographic system incorporating transportation and greenway trajectories (SC).

Courtyard building: A building that occupies the boundaries of its lot while internally defining one or more private patios (SC).

Curb: The edge of the vehicular pavement that may be raised or flush to a swale. It usually incorporates the drainage system (SC). Image: PBIC.

Curb extension: A section of sidewalk at an intersection or midblock crossing, which reduces the crossing width for pedestrians and which can help reduce traffic speeds. U.S. Dept. of Transportation. Image: PBIC.

Density: The number of dwelling units within a standard measure of land area (SC).

Diverter: A physical barrier that redirects traffic heading for a certain street onto a different course, reducing vehicle overload on vulnerable (usually residential) streets overrun by through traffic looking for shortcuts (PPS). Image: PPS-Boston, MA. Image ID 19492.

Edgeyard building: A building that occupies the center of its lot with setbacks on all sides (SC).

Façade: The exterior wall of a building that is set along a frontage line (SC).

Frontage: The area between a building façade and the vehicular lanes, inclusive of its built and planted components. Frontage is divided into private frontage and public frontage (SC).

Frontage line: A lot line bordering a public frontage. Façades facing frontage lines define the public realm and are therefore more regulated than the elevations facing other lot lines (SC).

Gateway: An entrance corridor that heralds the approach of a new landscape and defines the arrival point as a destination. A point along a roadway at which a motorist or pedestrian gains a sense of having entered the city or a particular part of the city. This impression can be imparted through such things as signs, monuments, landscaping, a change in development character, or a natural feature (PD). Image: PPS-ID 34739.

Green: A civic-space type for unstructured recreation, spatially defined by landscap¬ing rather than building frontages (SC).

Greenfield: An area that consists of open or wooded land or farmland that has not been previously developed (SC).

Greenway: An open space corridor in largely natural conditions, which may include trails for bicycles and pedestrians (SC). Image: PPS-Burlington Bikeway ID 40776.

Infill: (n.) new development on land that had been previously developed, includ¬ing most greyfield and brownfield sites, and cleared land within urbanized areas; (v.) to develop such areas (SC).

Kiosk: A freestanding structure upon which temporary information and posters, notices, and announcements are posted, or a freestanding building with one or more open sides from which commercial activities are conducted (PD). Image: PPS-Stockholm ID 47205.

Live-work: A mixed use unit consisting of a commercial and residential function. The commercial function may be anywhere in the unit. It is intended to be occupied by a business operator who lives in the same structure that contains the commercial activity or industry (SC).

Lot: A parcel of land accommodating a building or buildings of unified design. The size of a lot is controlled by its width in order to determine the grain (fine grain or coarse grain) of the urban fabric (SC).

Lot line: The boundary that legally and geometrically demarcates a lot (SC).

Lot width: The length of the principal frontage line of a lot. (SC).

Median: An area in the approximate center of a city street or state highway that is used to separate the directional flow of traffic. It may contain left-turn lanes, and is demarcated by curb and guttering, having painted or thermally applied stripes or other means to distinguish it from the portion of the roadway used for through traffic (PD). Image: PBIC.

Mixed use: Multiple functions within the same building through superimposition or adjacency, or in multiple buildings by adjacency, or at a proximity determined by warrant (SC).

Multigenerational park: A park that simultaneously provides outdoor physical activities and spaces for toddlers, children, teens, adults, and seniors. It includes both active (playground) and passive (leisure-time) activities, and may include equipment designed for multigenerational use. Image: PPS-ID 22165

Multiway boulevard: A street developed as two one-way pavements separated by a median (PD).

Neckdown: See choker.

Open space: Land intended to remain undeveloped; may be for civic space (SC).

Park: A civic-space type that is a natural preserve available for unstructured rec¬reation (SC). Image: PPS-St. Stephen's Green ID 37376.

Parking structure: A building containing one or more stories of parking above grade (SC). Image: PBIC.

Path: a pedestrian way traversing a park or rural area, with landscape matching the contiguous open space, ideally connecting directly with the urban sidewalk network (SC). Image: PPS-Parc Vallparadis Terrassa. Image ID 26446.

Pedestrian shed: An area that is centered on a common destination. Its size is related to average walking distances for the applicable community-unit type. Pedestrian sheds are applied to structure communities. A standard pedestrian shed is an average quarter-mile radius, or 1,320 feet, about the distance of a five-minute walk at a leisurely pace (SC).

Planter: The element of the public frontage that accommodates street trees, whether continuous or individual (SC). Image: PPS-Herald Square, New York. Image ID 43520.

Play lot: A small area developed especially for preschool or elementary school aged children. It may contain such facilities as sandboxes, slides, teeters, swings, and climbing apparatus (PD). Image: PPS-Luxembourg Gardens, Paris. Image ID 34175.

Plaza: A civic-space type designed for civic purposes and commercial activities in the more urban transect zones, generally paved and spatially defined by building frontages (SC). Image: PPS-Pioneer Courthouse, Portland. Image ID 22589.

Pocket park: A small area of open space that is developed and maintained for active or passive recreational use by the residents of a neighborhood or development. A pocket park may include lawn areas, a tot lot or playground, or picnic areas. Preservation of Undeveloped Land for Pocket Parks in Neighborhoods (2003). Image: PPS-ID 30653.

Principal building: The main building on a lot, usually located toward the frontage (SC).

Private frontage: The privately held layer between the frontage line and the principal building façade (SC).

Public frontage: The area between the curb of the vehicular lanes and the frontage line (SC).

Refuge island: A protected area between traffic lanes providing pedestrians with a safe place to wait for gaps in traffic. Glossary, St. Louis Great Streets Initiative. Image: PPS-ID 33049.

Right-of-way: (1) A strip of land acquired by reservation, dedication, prescription, or condemnation, and intended to be occupied by a street, trail, water line, sanitary sewer, and other public utilities or facilities; (2) the line determining the street or highway public limit or ownership; (3) a public or private area that allows for the passage of people or goods. Right-of-way includes passageways such as freeways, streets, bike paths, alleys, and walkways. A public right-of-way is a right-of-way that is dedicated or deeded to the public for public use and under the control of a public agency (PD).

Road: A local, rural, and suburban thoroughfare of low to moderate vehicular speed and capacity. This type is allocated to the more rural transect zones (T1–T3) (SC).

Roundabout: A raised island, which is usually landscaped and located at the intersection of two streets, used to reduce traffic speeds and accidents without diverting traffic onto adjacent residential streets (PD). Image: PBIC.

Row house: A single-family dwelling that shares a party wall with another of the same type and occupies the full frontage line (SC). Image: PPS-Boston, MA. Image ID 26814.

Setback: The area of a lot measured from the lot line to a building façade or elevation that is maintained clear of permanent structures, with the exception of encroachments (SC).

Sidewalk: The paved section of the public frontage dedicated exclusively to pedestrian activity (SC).

Sidewalk extension: See curb extension.

Square: A civic-space type designed for unstructured recreation and civic purposes, spatially defined by building frontages and consisting of paths, lawns, and trees, formally disposed (SC). Image: PPS-Manchester, England. Image ID 37290.
Street: A local urban thoroughfare of low speed and capacity (SC). Terminated vista: A location at the axial conclusion of a thoroughfare (SC).

Thoroughfare: A way for use by vehicular and pedestrian traffic and to provide access to lots and open spaces, consisting of vehicular lanes and the public frontage (SC).

Thoroughfare assembly: All the elements that surround and include thoroughfares: right-of-ways, parking lanes, travel lanes, curb radii, and public frontages (sidewalks, planters, street trees).

Traffic circle: See roundabout.

Transect: A cross section of the environment showing a range of different habitats. The rural-urban transect of the human environment used in the SmartCode template is divided into six transect zones. These zones describe the physical form and character of a place, according to the density and intensity of its land use and urbanism (SC).

Transect zone (T-zone): One of several areas on a zoning map regulated by the SmartCode. Transect zones are administratively similar to the land-use zones in conventional codes, except that, in addition to the usual building use, density, height, and setback requirements, other elements of the intended habitat are integrated, including those of the private lot and building and public frontage (SC).

Urbanism: Collective term for the condition of a compact, mixed use settlement, including the physical form of its development and its environmental, functional, economic, and sociocultural aspects (SC).

Woonerf: A Dutch word for an area, usually residential, where motorists and other users share the street without boundaries, such as lanes and curbs. The term can be translated as "residential yard," reflecting its popularity in the Netherlands where private space is limited. In a woonerf, people on bikes and on foot have access to the whole street, not just sidewalks. Moreover, the street functions as a public living room, where adults gather and children play safely because vehicle speed is kept to a minimum. (www.livablestreets.com/streetswiki/woonerf). Image: PBIC.

Zoning map: The official map or maps that are part of the zoning ordinance and delineate the boundaries of individual zones and districts (SC).

DISCUSSION QUESTIONS AND ACTIVITIES

Provided below is a list of questions and activities designed to help instructors working in a classroom setting expand on each topic and generate discussion. The exercises do not require any special software—just the Internet.

EXERCISE 1: NEIGHBORHOODS

The concept of "neighborhood" is a long-standing subject for sociologists and urban geographers, but is it a valid topic for urban designers? In what ways does the design of neighborhood form exclude people?

How can designers make sure the attempt to define and delimit neighborhoods does not exclude? Research Clarence Perry's ideas about the "neighborhood unit." Consult his original writing on the subject (Perry, 1929). Was his idea based on exclusion and social homogeneity, as is often assumed? What evidence is there for this? How does his proposed neighborhood unit design reflect this? Consult Banerjee and Baer's Beyond the Neighborhood Unit (1984) for a critique.

Research the debate over neighborhood form, particularly in terms of the placement and function of centers, edges, thoroughfares, and retail activities. Consult the neighborhood diagrams in Douglas Farr's Sustainable Urbanism and contrast with the alternatives shown in Duany, Plater-Zyberk and Company's Lexicon for the New Urbanism. In what specific ways do these designs differ? Contrast especially the placement of edges, retail, and "green" space.

Most residential neighborhoods in the United States are single use—housing only. How could design play a role in making neighborhoods more multi-use? Find examples of successful and unsuccessful neighborhood mixed-use, such as retail located within a residential neighborhood. What aspects of form, pattern, and other dimensions of design seem to be factors in differentiating between successful and unsuccessful commercial integration?

EXERCISE 2: TRANSECTS

Consult the research page of the Center for Applied Transect Studies (CATS) website (www.transect.org) and investigate the different ways in which transects have been portrayed. Some transects fall under the category "pop culture," and a few examples are shown here: www.transect.org/pop_img.html. There have also been transects of shoes, hairstyles, beverages, and cars. Devise your own transect categories for a given element and discuss how something seems to be more urban or more rural. How do such distinctions originate?

Find areas in your community that seem to exhibit a "transect violation"—that is, where an element of one kind of character seems inappropriately placed in a location of another type (i.e., a high-rise in a cornfield). Characterize the example and suggest an alternative location that you think would be more appropriate.

Go to the SmartCode website, www.smartcodecentral.com, and download a PDF of SmartCode Manual version 9.2. Find Table 4A, "Public Frontages." Walk down the main commercial street in your community—which will probably consist of T4, T5, or T6 zones—and photograph the frontages. Compare the frontages to the specifications in Table 4A and produce a map that indicates the lots that have frontages inappropriate for the T4, T5, or T6 zones. Would it make much of a difference to pedestrian life, commercial vitality, or the overall of quality of urbanism if the frontages were different? Think about what changes you would make.

EXERCISE 3: CONNECTIONS

What are the different ways urban environments connect people? Are there ways connections are made that have nothing to do with the physical environment or its design? If you said "the Internet," are you sure physical space is unrelated?

Review the different public and private frontage types shown in the SmartCode (www.smartcodecentral.org). Do you think some of these frontage types are better for connecting people than others?

Is connection always a good thing? Under what circumstances might an urban designer be interested in limiting connections? Can you find places in your community where there seems to be too much connectivity—for example, too many different pathways coming together?

EXERCISE 4: CENTERS

Go to the most popular corner in your community. (This is sometimes called the "100 percent corner.") Does this corner function like a center? What additional public spaces might be needed to help it become a true neighborhood center?

Do a Google map search on "centers" plus the name of your city or town. You will probably come up with a list of recreation centers, park centers, medical centers, and other "centers." Are any of these viable as community centers? Are they located in a way that makes sense for promoting them as "centers"?

Most communities have at least one publicly owned space termed a "community center" or "park and recreation center." Visit these spaces and think about their design. Are they welcoming and well connected? Are they accessible to pedestrians and bicyclists, or are they strictly car oriented? What possibilities do you see for improving their design?

Visit a location that you think holds the most promise as a unifying neighborhood center. Starting at the center, walk five minutes away from the center. Do this three or four times, each time in a different direction (or this could be assigned to a group). Each time, record the pedestrian quality of the routes linking the center to the surrounding area. What routes need to be better cared for, and what interventions would you propose?

EXERCISE 5: EDGES

Drive, bike, or walk along a major highway close to your community. How would you characterize the area immediately adjacent? Are there any areas that you think are successfully juxtaposed along the highway, or are the areas essentially write-offs that no one cares about? What design interventions can you come up with that would mitigate the harmful positioning of residential uses near strong edge conditions?

Find out where the official neighborhood boundaries are in your community, and drive, bike, or walk along them. Do they function like edges, or is the boundary purely an administrative artifact?

Go to a gated or walled community and observe how its edges function. What land uses surround the edges of the community? Is there any physical connection to surrounding areas? Are the residents justified in wanting to shield themselves off? Can you imagine interventions that would open up the gate or wall, at the entrance or elsewhere?

Visit the edge areas of an airport, hospital, campus, or other major institution or district. Characterize how the edges around them are treated. In what ways were these edges designed to consciously define and separate the surrounding area? Are they causing harm to surrounding areas? Do you think there are ways to improve them?

EXERCISE 6: MIX

Think about the limits of how mixed in use a neighborhood can be. Discuss how much mix you think your parents or grandparents would tolerate in their neighborhoods. In what specific ways can design help to alleviate concerns about mixing uses?

What uses should not be located near housing? Justify your selections, and consider whether your objections are intrinsically about the use or about how the use is typically designed.

In Google Earth or Google Maps (satellite view), look for areas in your community that appear to have a mix of housing types in the same small area (include several blocks). Visit these areas and characterize the mix—how are the housing types integrated? Do they face each other on a block, or do the block faces tend to be homogeneous? How do the units vary in terms of style, setbacks, height, materials, and rooflines?

EXERCISE 7: PROXIMITY

Go to www.walkscore.com, type in your address, and get the walkscore for your place of residence. Compare walkscores for the class. Do students who have high walkscores feel like they live in neighborhoods that are better designed than those in neighborhoods with lower walkscores?

Using census data by block or block group (www.census.gov), or based on your own knowledge of the local environment, find two types of areas in your city or town: low-income high density and high-income low density. Compare the walkscores for these two locations. You might want to summarize the scores for several points chosen from within the areas. How different are the scores?

Go to the www.socialexplorer.com and find the poorest census tract in your community. Make note of how many people live there, the percentages of different races, ethnicities, and education and income levels. Make note of the streets that bound the tract and then locate this area in a Google map. From Google, search on "groceries." What is the closest grocery store? Suggest closer locations, using an infill design for a small grocer. Consider designs from Natural Lawson (a Japanese grocer), Wild Oats, or Trader Joe's. Or, do an image search on "mom & pop grocers" for lots of good ideas.

EXERCISE 8: DENSITY

Find the part of your community that has the highest housing-unit or population density, according to census figures (use the census block geographic level). Find examples of this same level of density in Campoli and MacLean's book Visualizing Density, or visit the Lincoln Institute of Land Policy website for examples (www.lincolninst.edu/subcenters/visualizing-density). Determine which of their examples most closely matches the highest-density area of your community. Do their examples look much different? Characterize the differences.

Play the game "Building Blocks: A Density Game" as a classroom activity. Go to www.lincolninst.edu/subcenters/visualizing-density/blockgame/index.aspx to start the game. The game allows students to create their own neighborhood by arranging houses, streets, parks, parking units, and yards. Have each group create a low-, medium-, and high-density scenario. Compare and discuss the variation of results.

Ride the bus or take the light rail, depending on what you have access to. Working from the premise that density should be higher around a public transit stop, investigate places around stops where it appears density could go much higher. Working in teams, walk five minutes in all directions from a stop that has at least some existing commercial uses. Map out the infill possibilities for housing, including granny flats, duplexes, courtyard housing, or housing over commercial buildings. Compare notes and estimate how many units could be added.

EXERCISE 9: PARKING

Review the website www.parkingday.org for information about PARK(ing) Day, "a one-day, global event centered in San Francisco where artists, activists, and citizens collaborate to temporarily transform metered parking spots into 'PARK(ing)' spaces: temporary public parks." In your community, are there parking spaces, metered or otherwise, that could be turned into temporary public parks?

Select two places that you think represent clear examples of "good" and "bad" urbanism. Using Google Earth satellite imagery or simply visiting the area, count the number of parking spaces available in each location. Compare how parking in "good" and "bad" places differs.

Select a sample of parking garages in your community. Characterize and contrast the contexts of these structures. Do some structures seem to fit better with their surroundings than others? What seems to account for the difference?

Consider the ingress and egress of parking areas you know of, both surface lots and parking structures. Are there some access points that seem better designed than others? What factors account for this?

EXERCISE 10: TRAFFIC

Locate places in your community where traffic is particularly disruptive for pedestrians, such as a busy intersection, where pedestrians have to walk far or wait a long time to cross the street. Measure the street and determine whether the street could accommodate parking lanes, medians, or sidewalk extensions. Sketch out where your proposed interventions could go. How much do you think you could narrow the street?

Get a copy of The Boulevard Book by Jacobs, MacDonald, and Rofe (2001). It includes a compendium of multiway boulevards from around the world. Using Google Earth or Google Maps, find some of the boulevards discussed in the book. Select one, and sketch the basic outline of features: total width, lanes, parking, trees, medians, sidewalks, frontages. Make note of the direction of traffic. Can you imagine a section of street in your town that could accommodate these dimensions?

The website www.streetfilms.org contains many interesting short films on street-calming strategies and other creative ways to make cities more livable. Watch the videos on chicanes, raised crosswalks, and daylighting (removal of parking spaces near crosswalks). Create a map and use a legend to identify locations along busy streets you know of where you think these three strategies could work.

Take your redesigned street plans from any of the above to the local plan-review desk. (If you have access to a transportation planner, even better.) Get their review. Be prepared for rejection based on cost, safety, or impeded traffic flow. Come prepared with your rebuttal, and record the discussion.

INDEX

A

Access. See also proximity
    Kevin Lynch on, 79-81
Adobe Illustrator, 9

B

Buildings, types of, 8
Burden, Dan, 6

C

Centers
    commercial areas as, 57
    design strategies for, 53
    function of, 49
    parks as, 55
    schools as, 53
Chloropleth mapping, 89–90
Cité Industrielle, 101
Cognitive mapping, 22
Community-based urban design, 1,3
Connectivity, 35–45
    improving, 39-45
    Jane Jacobs and, 35
    problems with, 36,39
    scales of, 35-36

D

Density
    assumptions of, 89
    crowding and concentration, 87
    Jane Jacobs on, 87
    and transect zones, 89
    Increasing of, 87-90, 97

Design elements, 5-6
Dissect analysis, 27

E

Edges, defining of, 59-65
Emery, Mary, 93

F

First-tier suburbs, 10

G

Garden City designers, 89
Garnier, Tony, 101
Geographic information systems
    (GIS), 9

I

Incrementalism, 4
Infill strategies, 81
Institute for Transport Studies,
    University of Leeds, 101

J

Jacobs, Jane, 4
    on incrementalism, 4
    on connectivity, 35
    on crowding and concentration, 87
    on land use diversity, 69
    on parking, 93

K

Krier, Leon, 1

L

Land use
    diversity in, 69-76
Lynch, Kevin, 79-81

M

Mapping and spatial analysis, 9–10
Mariemont, Ohio, 93
Mix
    analysis, 15, 25-26, 28
    definition of, 47
    diversity in, 69
    low-density housing, 71-75
    policy and, 71
Morphology, 15–17
Mumford, Lewis
    on land-use diversity, 53

N

Neighborhood design 1-5
    centers in, 40–46
    characteristics of, 15
    cognitive delineation of, 22
    concepts of, 14–16
    density in, 66
    edges, defining of, 47–52
    land-use diversity in, 53–59
    parking's impact on, 71
    proximity in assessing, 61–63
    purposes of, 1
    social geography of, 39

Neighborhoods
    definition of, 22
New urbanists, 69,79
Nolen, John, 93

P
Parking, 85, 93-105
    and connectivity, 37-39
    in neighborhood centers, 53-57
    for promoting mix, 71-75
Parks
    in neighborhoods, 18-19, 23
    and the transect, 26-29
    and connectivity, 39,
    as neighborhood centers, 49-55
    proximity to, 79
Perry, Clarence, 7, 15, 17, 49
Photoshop, 9
Policies and programs
    impact on urban design, 5
    need for, 5
    as related to mix, 4
Portage Park
Chicago neighborhood, 10
    2000 census statistics of, 10
    central places in, 17-23, 50-55
    connectivity in, 38-39
    edges in, 59-65
    proximity to facilities in, 79-81
    transect zones in, 25-29, 89
    parking strategy in, 95-97
Proactive design, needs in, 4
Process-oriented urban design, 3
Project for Public Spaces, 6, 53, 102
Proximity, 79-82
    assessing use of, 69
    defining, 47
    identifying high-priority areas, 79-81
    proposing infill strategies for, 63
    in terms of access, 61
Public Lands Survey, 15
Public transit, 2, 10, 79, 89

Q
Quadrat, 27-30

R
Rybczynski, Witold, 1

S
Schools
    as neighborhood centers, 49-55
    in neighborhoods, 15, 17-18, 21
    for connectivity, 35, 41
    proximity to, 79
SketchUp, 8-10
SmartCode
    definition of, 8
    recommendations from, 25–32
Social objectives, 2–3
Software and data, 8-9
Street layout, 16
Suburbs,
    first tier, 10-11
    automobile, 93
Sustainability, 3
Synoptic survey, 25-27

T
3-D modeling, 9
3D Warehouse, 9
Tolman, Edward, 22
Traffic design strategies, 16.
    design strategies, 16, 85
    calming measures, 35, 41, 100-106
    designing thoroughfares, 103-105
    land-use separation in, 101
    pedestrian realm and, 96-97, 101
Transects, 25-33
    definition of, 13
    and density, 89-90
    and traffic, 103

U
Unwin, Raymond, 87, 89

Made in the USA
Middletown, DE
22 May 2022